ROUTLEDGE LIBRARY EDITIONS:
SAUDI ARABIA

Volume 3

SAUDI ARABIA

SAUDI ARABIA

MERI Report

MIDDLE EAST RESEARCH INSTITUTE

Routledge
Taylor & Francis Group
LONDON AND NEW YORK

First published in 1985

This edition first published in 2015
by Routledge
2 Park Square, Milton Park, Abingdon, Oxon, OX14 4RN

and by Routledge
711 Third Avenue, New York, NY 10017

Routledge is an imprint of the Taylor & Francis Group, an informa business

British Library Cataloguing in Publication Data
A catalogue record for this book is available from the British Library

ISBN: 978-1-138-82515-4 (Set)
ISBN: 978-1-138-84623-4 (Volume 3)

Publisher's Note
The publisher has gone to great lengths to ensure the quality of this reprint but points out that some imperfections in the original copies may be apparent.

Disclaimer
The publisher has made every effort to trace copyright holders and would welcome correspondence from those they have been unable to trace.

MERI REPORT

SAUDI ARABIA

Middle East Research Institute

CROOM HELM
London • Sydney • Dover, New Hampshire

Croom Helm Ltd, Provident House, Burrell Row,
Beckenham, Kent BR3 1AT

Croom Helm Australia Pty Ltd, First Floor,
139 King Street, Sydney, NSW 2001, Australia

British Library Cataloguing in Publication Data

Saudi Arabia. – (Meri report)
1. Saudi Arabia – Social conditions
I. University of Pennsylvania. *Middle East Research Institute* II. Series
958'.8053 HN663.A8

ISBN 0-7099-3545-5

Croom Helm, 51 Washington Street, Dover,
New Hampshire 03820, USA

Library of Congress Cataloging in Publication Data

University of Pennsylvania. Middle East Research
Institute.
MERI report, Saudi Arabia.

1. Saudi Arabia. 2. Saudi Arabia – Economic
conditions. I. Title: M.E.R.I. report,
Saudi Arabia.
DS204.U55 1985 330.953'8053 84-28553
ISBN 0-7099-3545-5 (pbk.)

Printed and bound in Great Britain by
Antony Rowe Ltd., Chippenham

TABLE OF CONTENTS

I. Background

1. Geography 3
2. Climate 3
3. Population 4
4. Resources 4
5. Social Structure 5
6. Military 6
7. Economic Structure 7
8. Infrastructure 7
9. Social Services 8
10. Foreign Relations 8

II. Political Analysis

1. Political Structure 13
   1.1 Political Institutions 13
   1.2 Political Leadership 14
   1.3 The Role of the Military 15
   1.4 The Role of Religion 16
      The Wahhabi Revival of Islam 16
      Islam Today 16
      World View 17
   1.5 Regional and Tribal Differences 18
   1.6 Political Opposition 19
      The Grand Mosque Takeover 19
      Shiite Opposition 21
      Palestinians 22
   1.7 Political Economy 22
      The Private Sector 22
      The Public Sector 23
      Manpower Shortages 23
      Domestic and Foreign Investment 24
      Education and Social Change 24
      Women's Education 25
   1.8 Factors for Stability and Instability 26

2. Recent Developments: 1975-1984

   2.1 Internal Developments—Political 29
   2.2 Economic 30
   2.3 Revenue Reduction 31

3. External Developments

3.1 Saudi Strategy 33
3.2 The Arab/Israeli Problem 33
3.3 The Islamic World 34
3.4 Relations with South Arabia 34
3.5 Relations with Egypt 35
3.6 Relations with Jordan, Iraq and Syria 36
3.7 Relations with Israel 36
3.8 The PLO 37
3.9 Lebanon 38
3.10 Relations with non-Arab Muslim Countries 38
3.11 The Iran-Iraq War 39
3.12 The West 40
3.13 Western Europe and Japan 41
3.14 The Communist World 41
3.15 The Third World 42

4. Present Situation

4.1 Internal 43
4.2 External 44

5. Future Prospects

5.1 Time of Tension 45
5.2 Domestic Policy 45
5.3 U.S. Saudi Relations 46
5.4 Relations with the Arab States 46
5.5 Islamic World 46
5.6 Toward a New Consensus 46

III. Economic Analysis

1. Summary Conclusions 49
1.1 GDP Growth 49
1.2 Sectoral Breakdown of GDP 49
1.3 Economic Planning 49
1.4 Public Policy 49
1.5 The Oil Sector 50
1.6 The Agriculture Sector 50
1.7 Manufacturing Sector 50
1.8 Manpower 50
1.9 The Financial Sector 50
1.10 Balance of Payments 51

2. Macro Economic Analysis
2.1 Recent Developments: Structural Changes 53
2.2 The Petroleum Sector (1969-1978) 54
2.3 State of the Economy (1978/79-1980/81) 54
2.4 Recent Developments 55
2.5 Short-term Outlook 57
2.6 Sectoral Breakdown 59

3. Development Planning and Public Policy
3.1 The First Development Plan (1970-1974) 61
3.2 The Second Development Plan (1975-1980) 61
3.3 The Third Development Plan (1980-1985) 62
3.4 Assessment of Performance 62
3.5 The Fourth Plan (1985/86-1990/91) 64
3.6 The Budget 65

4. Petroleum Sector
4.1 Saudi Oil Reserves 69
4.2 Gas Reserves 69
4.3 Development and Organization of the Oil and Gas Industry 70
4.4 Production and Pricing Policies: Strengths and Constraints 71
4.5 Production and Pricing: The Record 73
4.6 Consumption of Energy 74
4.7 Oil and Gas-Related Industries 75

5. Agriculture Sector
5.1 Current Conditions 77
5.2 Constraints on Development 78
5.3 Government Support 80
5.4 Crop Distribution 82
5.5 Livestock and Fisheries 82

6. Industrial Sector
6.1 General Conditions 85
6.2 Expansion 85
6.3 Problems and Constraints 86
6.4 Incentives for Private Sector Investment 88
6.5 Existing Industries 89

7. Manpower
7.1 Serious Shortages 91
7.2 Foreign Workers 91
7.3 Treatment of Foreigners 93
7.4 Training Programs 94

7.5 The Role of Women 95
7.6 Distribution of Employment by Sector 96
7.7 Prospects 97

8. Finance
8.1 Deceleration in the Money Supply 99
8.2 The Saudi Arabian Monetary Agency 100
8.3 Commercial Banks 102
8.4 Bank Credit 103
8.5 Other Financial Institutions 104
8.6 Islamic Banking 104

9. Construction
9.1 General Conditions 107
9.2 Growth of Construction 107
9.3 Adverse Developments 108
9.4 Current Conditions and Prospects 109

10.1 Balance of Payments
10.1 Exports 113
10.2 Imports 114
10.3 Current Account 115
10.4 Capital Account 116
10.5 Foreign Aid 116

IV. Saudi Arabia Statistical Appendix

Table 1. Basic Information 121
Table 2. Official Calendar of Saudi Arabia 122
Table 3. Cabinet List 123

Defense

Table 4. Trade in Major Conventional Weapons 126
Table 5. U.S. Arms Transfers to Saudi Arabia 128
Table 6. Saudi Arabia Military Personnel and Equipment 129

Water Resources

Table 7. Highlights of the Plan for Water Development 134
Table 8. Water Resources and Demand: 1980-2000 136

Demography

Table 9.	Basic Indicators	138
Table 10.	Population of Major Cities	138

Economy

Table 11.	Major Economic Indicators	140
Table 12.	Cost of Living Indices	140
Table 13.	GDP at Constant Prices	141

Banking and Finance

Table 14.	Financial Survey	144
Table 15.	Leading Saudi Banks	145
Table 16.	Commercial Bank Credit by Sector	145
Table 17.	Commercial Banks: Assets and Liabilities	146
Table 18.	Exchange Rates	

Budget and Planning

Table 19.	Budget Estimates	148
Table 20.	Budget Allocation by Sector	149
Table 21.	Saudi Budget (1984-1985)	150

Economic Assistance

Table 22.	Allocations of Saudi Foreign Aid	152

Energy

Table 23.	Energy Outlook	156
Table 24.	Energy Supply and Demand	156
Table 25.	Crude Oil Production	157
Table 26.	Saudi Oil Concessions	157
Table 27.	Oil Exports by Company	157
Table 28.	Crude Petroleum Exports by Destination	158
Table 29.	Crude Oil Prices	158
Table 30.	Production of Petroleum Products	159
Table 31.	Domestic Consumption of Refined Petroleum Products	159
Table 32.	Electric Utility Industry Energy Sales and Consumption	160
Table 33.	Electric Utility Industry Peak Load Installed Capacity	160

Industry

Table 34. SABIC: Domestic Heavy Industry Projects 162
Table 35. Value of SIDF-Approved Industrial Loans by Sector 163

Agriculture and Fishing

Table 36. Area Planted and Production of Main Crops 166
Table 37. Livestock Product Production, Imports & Consumption 168
Table 38. Live Animals

Trade

Table 39. Balance of Payments 172
Table 40. Trade by Commodity Sector 173
Table 41. Commodity Composition of Imports 173
Table 42. Direction of Trade($) 174
Table 43. Foreign Trade Indicators 175
Table 44. Direction of Trade(%) 175

Labor

Table 45. Employment by Sector 178
Table 46. Distribution of Employment by Economic Activity 178
Table 47. Civilian Employment 179
Table 48. Composition of the Labor Force 179

Transportation & Communications

Table 49. Transportation Infrastructure 182
Table 50. Saudia Fleet 182
Table 51. Volume of Passengers at International Airports 183
Table 52. Tourism 183
Table 53. Total Cargo at the International Airports 183
Table 54. Ports and Shipping 184
Table 55. Telephones in the Kingdom 184
Table 56. Principal Daily Newspapers 185
Table 57. Radio and Television Broadcasting 185

Health, Education and Welfare

Table 58. Health Facilities in the Kingdom 188

Table 59. Enrollment in Educational Institutions 188

Table 60. Schools, Teachers, and Pupils in Saudi Arabia 189

I. BACKGROUND

1. GEOGRAPHY. The Kingdom of Saudi Arabia occupies four-fifths of the Arabian Peninsula, although the size of the country cannot be fixed precisely because most of its southern borders are undemarcated. Its area is approximately 2,150,260 sq km (1 sq km = 0.386 sq mi). Bounded on the east by the Persian (Arabian) Gulf and on the west by the Red Sea, on the north by Jordan, Iraq and Kuwait, and on the south and southeast by the Yemens, Oman, the United Arab Emirates and Qatar, Saudi Arabia extends in a rough rectangle 1,600 km from east to west and 1,920 km from north to south (1 km = 0.62 mi).

Topographically, as well as geologically, Saudi Arabia is tilted up on the Red Sea side where the mountains of the Hijaz and the Asir rise to 3,050 m (1 m = 3.28 ft). These mountains form an escarpment rising abruptly from Tihama, the Red Sea coastal plain, sloping gently eastward to sea level at the Persian Gulf. Central Arabia, called Najd, is a mostly arid plain broken by occasional oases. It is dissected from north to south by a second westward-facing escarpment, Jabal Tuwayq, which extends over 960 km north to south. At the southern end, it runs into the vast Rub al-Khali, or Empty Quarter, the world's largest sand desert, where dunes of pink quartz sand rise 244 m from the desert floor.

2. CLIMATE. Virtually the entire country is desert except for the highlands of the Hijaz and Asir, and even there droughts can last for several years. The rapidly growing capital, Riyadh, survives only on water mined from non-replenishable aquifers of fossil water. The temperatures are extreme, exceeding 45° C (130° F) in the interior during the summer months. In the coastal areas, temperatures are lower, but the climate is far more uncomfortable and the humidity prevents the temperature from dropping at night. By contrast, the dry interior can witness a temperature drop of over 28° C (50° F) within a few hours after sunset and in winter can drop below freezing. In the mountains of Asir to the west, sufficient rain falls for some dry farming. In the north, it rains 100-200 mm annually (1 mm = 0.039 inch), while in the south several years may pass between rainfalls, and only oases and wells provide water. The largest oasis in the world, Hasa (al-Hasa), is located in the Eastern Province and is the site of extensive agricultural reclamation projects.

3. POPULATION. There are no exact population figures for Saudi Arabia. Estimates range from less than five million native population to over eight million. The current figure, which includes foreign residents, is 9.3 million. UN sources estimate that the population is increasing at a rapid rate, 3.6 percent annually. There are probably one to two million resident aliens, close to half from North Yemen. Saudi Arabia does not have a single dominant metropolis such as Cairo or Baghdad. But its major cities are expanding; and some sources state that in 1980 approximately 67 percent of the population lived in urban areas. Jeddah, on the Red Sea, and Riyadh, the capital, are approaching one million. Other urban centers are Mecca and Medina in the Hijaz and Dammam in the Eastern Province. Two new industrial cities, Jubayl and Yanbu, have been built as industrial centers and military fortifications.

4. RESOURCES. Geologically, the mountains of Hijaz and Asir comprise one of the few areas in the world where the oldest geological stratum, called the pre-Cambrian shield or basement complex, is found exposed. Farther east, the stratum is buried under sedimentary layers formed when eastern Arabia was part of a vast ancient sea, of which the Persian Gulf is the last remnant. Plant and animal deposits from the ancient sea, trapped under great pressure domes or anticlines in the downward sloping strata, are the source of the region's vast oil deposits.

The discovery of oil in the 1930s has vastly changed the economic and social fabric of the Kingdom. With proven oil reserves of 162.4 billion barrels (probable reserves raise that figure to 250 billion barrels) and 1983 production at 5.05 mbd, Saudi Arabia possesses about one-fourth of the world's oil reserves, is the third greatest oil producer (after the USSR and the United States), and the world's largest oil exporter.

With the exception of its massive oil and natural gas reserves, Saudi Arabia has few other natural resources. Phosphate deposits in the Wadi Sirhan on the Jordanian border might be of sufficient quantity to make them economically attractive. Since the rise in the price of gold in recent years, that metal is being extracted in modest quantities. There are other mineral deposits, including iron, but none as yet have been found in commercial quantities.

Saudi Arabia has engaged in commercial fishing in the Persian Gulf. Although considerable potential also exists in the Red Sea, little has been done to exploit it.

Given the lack of rainfall, groundwater, permanent rivers or bodies of water, the country relies on scarce surface water and on desalination plants to meet its water needs. In 1983, these plants desalinated 1.89 million cu m of water. At present, less than 1 percent of the land is cultivated, but studies have shown that the area of cultivable land could be increased significantly. The government has completed several land reclamation and dry-farming projects and is planning several more.

5. SOCIAL STRUCTURE. Despite the barrage of foreign ideas, techniques and technology Saudi Arabia is still a highly traditional Islamic society. Education, mass media and the influences of modernization have certainly changed expectations in Saudi Arabia but have not created the kind of identity crisis prevalent in other developing countries. Saudis know who they are. This strong sense of identity is based upon strong family ties and historical factors.

Unlike most of the Arab world, Saudis have never been subject to foreign rule. The only time in recent history when Central Arabia has been under foreign domination was in 1818 when a Turkish-Egyptian force under Ibrahim Pasha occupied and destroyed the capital at Diriyyah. Four years later, the force departed and the Saudis rebuilt their capital at Riyadh, a few miles to the south. Saudi identification with pan-Arabism and pan-Islamism is also very different from many of their Arab neighbors. For the former, Arabism is more a matter of Arabian bloodlines than the self-conscious rediscovery of historic Arab glory and the conscious attempt to restore pride lost under foreign imperialism. As for pan-Islam, the Wahhabi revival began in the mid-18th century, a full century before pan-Islamism became a popular ideology elsewhere. Indeed, it was the spiritual leadership of Muhammad bin Abd al-Wahhab, the revival's founder, and the temporal leadership of his patron, Muhammad bin Saud, founder of the Saudi dynasty, which began the process of consolidation which culminated in the present Kingdom. These two distinctive elements of Saudi heritage, Arabism and Islam, are basic to the sense of identity within Saudi society.

The homogenous composition of the population is another factor contributing to the Saudi identity. Most Saudis are Arab Sunni Muslims. The only significant indigenous minority group is the Shiite Muslim community of the Eastern Province, found mainly in the oases of Qatif and Hasa.

The extended family remains the core of Saudi society, with several members of an extended family usually living together in a single compound. It is common for first cousins to marry and rare that marriages occur among families of unequal status.

The role of women in traditional Saudi society does not fit Western stereotypes. Although women have almost no independent mobility outside the home, are usually veiled in public, and are physically segregated from the world of men, within the extended family women have considerable power and a wife may draw upon support from other female family members to exert her influence. Since 1960, when schools were first opened to women, increasing numbers of Saudi women have attained higher degrees. Over 50 percent of the female population in the primary school age group are enrolled in educational institutions compared to 64 percent of the male population in a similar category. Saudis are just beginning to tap the economic resource of women workers, especially in technical fields where labor needs are greatest. Though progress will be slow it is inevitable that Saudi women will become more active in Saudi society than they have been allowed to be in the past. They are not likely to follow Western patterns of integration but will define their own paths consistent with their cultural and religious heritage.

6. MILITARY. The armed forces in Saudi Arabia number 76,500, including an active National Guard force of about 25,000. All branches of the military are undergoing a modernization program, but despite advanced weaponry and training, the Saudi armed forces are not thought capable of defending the Kingdom against a large invasion force. This is in part due to the fact that the Royal Family has kept both forces small, since it is well aware that many Third World regimes are overthrown by their armed forces. To guard against this, a number of younger princes have been encouraged to have military careers, and the government spends considerable amounts on military infrastructure and equipment to insure the loyalty of the armed forces.

Saudi Arabia's spending for defense and military manpower increased from $20.7 billion in 1980 to $27.02 billion in 1982 and dropped back to $21.9 billion in 1983/84. This figure represents 30.7 percent of the Saudi budget. The increasingly sophisticated equipment used by the Saudi armed forces will necessitate more advanced training programs for Saudi military personnel boosting defense expenditures even further in the future.

7. ECONOMIC STRUCTURE. Saudi Arabia pursues a form of Islamic capitalism which, by Western standards, is very free-wheeling, with a strong emphasis on private property and private wealth. However, the public sector dominates the economy and oil dominates the public sector. Oil revenues yield something over $50 billion per year, down from the more than $100 billion of 1981 because of the oil glut. The Kingdom's $125 billion in foreign exchange holdings provide a secure cushion and generate considerable income. Revenue shortfall has necessitated some drawdown in reserves, cancellation of some projects and stretching out of others. Nevertheless, strains are manageable and the enforced slowdown in spending may have social and political benefits after a period of what many considered to be excessively rapid development.

8. INFRASTRUCTURE. Under the Second Five Year Plan, corresponding to the latter half of the 1970s, massive spending was devoted to development of the country's physical infrastructure as under the First Plan. While it was necessary to take anti-inflation measures in 1978, curtailing somewhat the pace of development, the results were impressive – a tripling of paved highway mileage, a tenfold expansion of seaport capacity, and an increase in power generation by a multiple of twenty-eight.

The transportation industry is one of the fastest growing industries in Saudi Arabia, with growth rates approaching 20 percent annually in some instances. The great distances and difficult terrain have made aviation the most important element in the transportation industry. There are 24 airports throughout the Kingdom. The national air carrier, Saudia, is one of the largest in the Middle East, and services numerous domestic and international cities, providing both passenger and cargo services. Saudia is the largest employer in Saudi Arabia after the ARAMCO oil company and the government. Some $2 billion were allocated to Saudia under the Third Plan, much of which will be used to acquire new aircraft. In

1983, it carried nine million international and eleven million domestic passengers.

Saudi Arabia's road system has improved dramatically over the past decades. In the 1950s, Saudi Arabia had less than 240 km of roads; now it has more than 28,000 km of asphalted roads, and 29,000 of agricultural roads with more expansion projected under the new Plan, including a six-lane Mecca-Medina highway and a transpeninsular expressway. The road system connects all but the most remote areas, a factor that should encourage the development of trucking as an alternative means for transporting goods internally. Although presently there are only 577 km of single track railroad between Dammam and Riyadh, with an additional 170 km of spur lines, expansion is contemplated, including the reconstruction of the Hijaz line between Medina and Amman, blown up in World War I.

A comprehensive telecommunications system – possibly the best in the world – has been installed in Saudi Arabia. By the end of 1983, Saudi Arabia had 807,000 telephone lines and 16,044 telex lines, with further expansion planned. Saudi Arabia is also a major owner of Arabsat, an international communications system.

9. SOCIAL SERVICES. Education, which is free to all Saudi citizens, is encouraged but not compulsory. In fiscal year 1983/84, 10.6 percent of the budget was allocated for human resources. Sixty-four percent of the population (male and female) aged five to nineteen goes to school. There are seven universities for men and seven colleges for women, as well as specialized institutions for religious studies, for technical training, for the handicapped, and for increasing adult literacy. Nonetheless, the literacy rate is still relatively high; in 1980, 87.8 percent of the female and 65.5 percent of the male population over 15 were illiterate.

The development of a modern health care system began more than a decade ago. Health services in the Kingdom surpass those of any other state in the region. Health care expenditure represents the third largest budget allocation (after defense and education). The Third Plan (1980-1985) envisages the construction of 36 new hospitals and 320 regional health care centers. At year-end 1982, there were already 117 hospitals with a capacity of 23,500 beds. Training of medical personnel is also a priority.

10. FOREIGN RELATIONS. Historically, Saudi foreign policy has been determined primarily by three factors: geographic location, Islamic world view, and the need for consensus in decisionmaking within the Royal Family.

Fear of encirclement is typical of many insular or peninsular nations. Historically, the Saudis have feared any regimes with rival claims to legitimacy, such as the Hashemite monarchy of Jordan until a 1960s rapprochement. Nasser's secular Arab nationalism was particularly threatening in the 1960s while Egypt supported the republican factions in the Yemen. In the late 1970s, the Saudis saw a threat in the military modernization of the Shah's Iran. This military buildup, together with resurgent Shiite Islam, has made Iran the most important challenger to Saudi security and continued rule by the House of Saud.

According to Islam the World is divided into those living under God's law (Dar al-Islam), and those living outside God's law (Dar al-Harb). Islam recognizes Christianity and Judaism as revealed religions and accepts adherents to those theologies as living under the law. For Saudi policy makers, Dar al-Islam roughly approximates the free world and Dar al-Harb approximates the atheist communist world. Hence, the Soviet bloc is the greatest international threat. The Saudis also distinguish between Judaism, a monotheistic religion, and Zionism, an alien political doctrine and an immediate threat because it divides the free world and dissipates Muslim energy.

The third feature of Saudi foreign policy is the decisionmaking process within the Royal Family. Saudi pragmatism and conservatism are the end result of consensus among factions as to what is politically acceptable.

II. POLITICAL ANALYSIS

1
POLITICAL STRUCTURE

1.1 POLITICAL INSTITUTIONS. At the time Abd al-Aziz (known in the West as Ibn Saud) began to consolidate his hold over the present-day Kingdom in the first quarter of this century, there were no formal political institutions in the Western sense. After conquest of the Hijaz in the 1920s, Hijazi government institutions were gradually absorbed into the nascent national government. Beginning with the creation of the Ministry of Finance in 1930 and the Ministry of Foreign Affairs in 1932, ministries appeared until, by the death of King Abd al-Aziz in 1953, the first Saudi Council of Ministers was created.

In the absence of a legislature, the Council of Ministers combines many of the legislative as well as executive features found in Western governments. In addition, there exist a number of special commissions and councils (such as the Royal Commission for Jubayl and Yanbu, and the Supreme Petroleum Council) which are charged with specific responsibilities. Because many of the ministries predate the creation of the Council of Minsters, the separate ministries have retained significant powers within their spheres of influence.

Saudi government has always been more person-oriented than position-oriented. Two of the most important aspects of government operation are the twin principles of "consensus" (ijma) and "consultation" (shura). The concept of "desert democracy," often heard in conjunction with Saudi Arabia, is bound up in these terms. Ideally, after consultation with as wide a group of knowledgeable people as possible, a consensus is created, and decisions are made on the basis of this consensus. Because the process is informal, it can be carried on anywhere and include anyone who holds a position of trust. The King's public majlis (literally a sitting or an assembly, used here to mean holding a public audience), the audiences of princes and other national and regional leaders, private dinners – all these can be part of the exercise of shura and ijma.

There is currently a commission studying plans for a Consultative Assembly (not a full legislature, for in

Islamic law, only God can legislate, and law is sacred), and a reform of provincial government. These measures, though long discussed, are apparently being held in abeyance, very probably by opposition from the religious establishment whose authority would be diluted.

1.2 POLITICAL LEADERSHIP. The Saudi political leadership is dominated by the House of Saud. No one knows exactly how large the royal family is, but estimates exceed 2,000. The King is the head of the family as well as chief of state and head of government. Because of the absence of a system of formal checks and balances (other than Islamic law), it is often (and erroneously) assumed that he is an absolute monarch. This assumption fails to take into account the role of the family, which serves as the political constituency of the Kingdom. Without its support, no man can remain king. For example, when King Saud lost the support of the family in 1964, he was replaced by his brother King Faisal.

Though closely related, royal family politics and national politics are different. Standing in the family depends to a large extent on generation and branch of the family. For example, the second ranking prince after the King is Muhammad Saud al-Kabir, head of a senior but less prominent branch.

Politically, the sons of King Abd al-Aziz are the most prominent, but political standing also requires leadership ability. Members of this group of the royal family hold all the national security-related portfolios. After Kind Fahd, the most politically visible princes are Prince Abdallah, Crown Prince and head of the National Guard; Prince Sultan, Defense Minister; Prince Nayif, Interior Minister; and Prince Salman, Governor of Riyadh. All but Abdallah are blood brothers (the Sudairi Seven), which adds to their propensity to work in concert.

A number of second generation princes (grandsons of King Abd al-Aziz) are beginning to enter public life. They include the Foreign Minister, Prince Saud bin Faisal; Intelligence Chief, Prince Turki bin Faisal (both sons of the late King Faisal); and Ambassador to the United States, Prince Bandar bin Sultan. Though growing in prestige, their status as a younger generation will never enable them to compete for influence on equal terms with their uncles.

The second leadership group is comprised of the technocrats who serve throughout the government. The Saudi royal family appoints qualified people to technically demanding positions, with the result that there are more

Ph.D.s at the cabinet level in Saudi Arabia than in the United States. Among the leading technocrats are Petroleum Minister Zaki Yamani, Finance Minister Muhammad Aba al-Khayl (perhaps the most influential commoner in the government), and Planning Minister Hisham Nazir.

1.3 THE ROLE OF THE MILITARY. Saudi Arabia is one of very few countries in the Middle East in which the military has not played a significant role in politics. It is true that Abd al-Aziz used a tribal force of Islamic zealots, the Ikhwan, to consolidate the Kingdom, but after an uprising in 1929, the Ikhwan were disbanded and Saudi Arabia had no regular military force until after World War II.

In 1945 King Abd al-Aziz concluded an agreement with the United States to build an air field and related facilities at Dhahran, to which the United States would have access, and to help train a Saudi air force. In 1951 the United States Military Training Mission (USMTM) was established to help train all branches of the Saudi armed forces. There was still ambivalence on the part of the Saudis about developing the armed forces. All around them, monarchies were being replaced by military dictatorships. During the 1960s and 1970s, the Saudis realized that they could not get along without a modern military establishement. The June 1967 Arab-Israeli War convinced them that Saudi troops would have to be available and acquit themselves reasonably well in another war with Israel, or the Kingdom would face dire domestic as well as external political consequences. Moreover, in 1971, the British withdrew from the Gulf; by the late 1970s, communism was spreading in the Horn of Africa and South Asia; and, in 1978, the Shah's regime collapsed in Iran. During this period the Saudis saw no alternative to major military development. Still, ambivalence remains. One reason for elaborate spending on military infrastructure and equipment is to insure the loyalty of the armed forces. It is also in part why the younger princes are encouraged to undertake military careers.

The Iran-Iraq war, which began in September 1980, has created a new urgency for developing the capabilities of the military and the independent, tribally-based National Guard. Modernization for both has been primarily in the hands of the United States. As matters stand (and despite the downing of an Iranian fighter in June 1984), Saudi Arabia has virtually no capability to counter a conventional air, sea, or land attack on its oil facilities. The United States' willingness to lease and ultimately sell AWACS radar aircraft was in part a response to the need to defend the oil fields. The effort by the U.S. President to win Senate approval for the sale was greatly appreciated by the Saudis, and should enhance joint U.S.-Saudi cooperation in defense matters. Nevertheless, the effort the White House had to expend to gain approval of the AWACS deal raised doubts among key Saudis about American reliability in the face of Israeli opposition. This has led gradually to a more independent Saudi Middle East policy, less inclined to serve American interests automatically, and with a greater sensitivity to the political cost of having too close ties to the Americans.

1.4 THE ROLE OF RELIGION. Throughout the Middle East, Islam is more than a religion; it is a way of life, making little distinction between secular and sacred. However, historical and doctrinal circumstances in each country determine the role of religion in politics and society. In Saudi Arabia, Islam provides the political ideology of the regime as well as the constitutional base for the legal system. Islamic law (or Sharia) is the official law of the land.

The Wahhabi Revival of Islam. Many Saudis adhere to the austere Hanbali school of Islamic jurisprudence, as interpreted in the 18th century by Islamic reformer Muhammad bin Abd al-Wahhab. Wahhab was critical of "innovations" (bida) which, he felt, had distorted Islam over the centuries, such as Shiite veneration of saints or popular Sufi rituals. At the same time, he advocated "reopening the door of ijtihad" (personal interpretation by Islamic scholars) to give them the freedom to use reason to interpret Islamic law in the light of changing circumstances. This type of interpretation had been forbidden by Islamic scholars in the ninth and tenth centuries, meaning that the law remained unchanged although societies throughout the Muslim world had changed dramatically in the thousand years since the advent of Islam.

Ibn Abd al-Wahhab was allied by marriage with the founder of the Saud dynasty, who was committed to military achievement of Ibn Abd al-Wahhab's religious ideals. Several generations later, the Saudi-Wahhabi alliance culminated in the conquests of Abd al-Aziz Ibn Saud, from which was born the Kingdom of Saudi Arabia.

Islam Today. The descendants of Muhammad bin Abd al-Wahhab have considerable influence in the Kingdom. The Minister of Justice, who after the King is the principal judicial officer, is from Al Shaikh, the family of descendants of Muhammad bin Abd al-Wahhab. Religious leaders (ulama) use their kinship to the Royal Family to oppose innovations which they regard as contrary to Islam. In the time of Ibn Saud, this included opposition to photography, the telephone, and education of women. In each case, the king succeeded in convincing the leaders that what seemed like an innovation actually had an Islamic purpose. More recently, the ulama have opposed as corrupting influences the introduction of television, the employment of women, and the extensive program of modernization. In 1965 members of the Royal Family, some from the Shammari tribe in the north, stormed a Jeddah television station. Ten years later, the mentally unbalanced brother of one of the victims of that incident assassinated King Faisal.

Islam plays a major role in public administration, in foreign policy, and in commerce. One of the largest single exercises in public administration anywhere is the annual Hajj. Because 2.5 million pilgrims (roughly half from outside the Kingdom) attend each year, overseeing the provision of food, water, health, sanitation, transportation, and instruction on the Hajj rites requires virtually the entire resources of the Saudi government. One reason Saudi Arabia has never adopted a fiscal year on the solar calendar (eleven days longer than the Islamic lunar calendar that governs the scheduling of the Hajj) is that at some point it would require getting out the government's budget and administering the Hajj at the same time, a sheer impossibility.

World View. In their foreign policy, the Saudi's draw heavily on the classical Islamic world view. Although Islam is considered the last and final revelation of God's law, Muslims recognize Christianity and Judaism as revealed religions, and accept their adherents as "Peoples of the Book." There is a clear preference for the Christian west over the atheistic communist east. This is an important component of Saudi relations with the United States and Western Europe. In addition, the Saudis predilection for free enterprise implies extensive ties with the capitalist nations.

Saudis feel a special responsibility for the protection of Islamic values. Islam originated in Arabia, the language of the Quran is Arabic, and the two holiest sites in Islam (Mecca and Medina) are located in Saudi Arabia. The perceived role as leader in the Muslim World influences almost all foreign policy decisions.

1.5 REGIONAL AND TRIBAL DIFFERENCES. There are pronounced regional differences in Saudi Arabia, the main one being the contrast between (1) the desert interior, (2) the cosmopolitan port cities and pilgrimage sites, and (3) the technological oil centers of the eastern province.

In the interior, the Nejdis of Riyadh led by the House of Saud, were the political consolidators of the Kingdom. The Rashidis of Hail, part of the Shammar confederation, were the last tribe to be subdued and have never quite accepted their subordinate position. To ensure docility after the 1921 fall of Hail, Abd al-Aziz invited the vanquished princes of Hail to live at his court. He also married the widow of a prominent Rashidi, Fahadah bint Asi al-Shuraym. The only issue of that union was Abdallah, the present Crown Prince. This was one of a series of political marriages by Ibn Saud that cemented the strategic tribal alliances upon which the Kingdom and the royal family are built.

In contrast to the interior, where lineage and values remained constant due to isolation, the cities of the western coast – Jeddah, Mecca and Medina in the Hijaz – are more sophisticated. Historically, Hijazis have married foreigners from all corners of the Muslim World and received a heavy infusion of Turkish stock during the Ottoman Empire. Mecca and Medina are the holy cities, centers of pilgrimage and religious learning; they receive an influx of Muslims from around the world, over a million annually. Although permanent migration is no longer allowed the sociological impact of years of influx has left its mark on the population. Hosting the Hajjis gave rise to a number of prominent and politically important merchant families which still dominate commerce in the Kingdom.

Jeddah, the seat of the Foreign ministry and foreign embassies, is the center of trade and commerce and the city most hospitable to foreigners.

The third important region is the Eastern Province, which before the days of oil was dominated by its large oases, al-Hasa and Qatif, both with sizeable Shiite Muslim populations. Since the discovery of oil in the 1930s, the Eastern Province has become more cosmopolitan, drawing people from all over the Kingdom and all over the world. The bulk of Saudi Arabia's large resident alien population is found here. For years the Arab American Oil Company (ARAMCO) and its subcontractors employed a majority of foreign workers, but, as Saudi Arabia has begun to implement its saudisation program and given priority to industrial development and diversification, this is no longer so.

The Saudi Arabian Monetary Agency (SAMA) is located in Jeddah. From SAMA emanate the orders to ARAMCO telling where to deposit the oil revenues, huge amounts of which are cleared through Chase Manhattan, Morgan Guaranty, and Citibank, among others. Banking retainers from the USA, Britain, and Switzerland are a fixture of the Kandara Palace Hotel in Jeddah; nearly all Saudi men who matter in Jeddah spend some time in the Kadara Palace lobby each week.

Tribalism is the tarp on which Saudi society has been woven. Ibn Saud's policy of political marriages with minor and major tribes created singlehandedly a network that today numbers 3,000-5,000 princes. But the stress of rapid social mobilization, combined with Western influence and petrodollars, is weakening that network.

1.6 POLITICAL OPPOSITION. Political parties are forbidden in Saudi Arabia, as is any criticism of the Royal Family. On the surface, there appears to be little opposition to government policies. However, there are actually two levels of opposition: within the Royal Family, and outside of it.

Within the Royal Family there is debate among factions: western-oriented, pan-Arab, religious. A consensus is forged, and the Family closes ranks behind the consensus. Only rarely does internal debate surface as open opposition. In 1969 several Saudi princes defected to Egypt under the influence of Nasser.

Outside the family, during the 1960s and 1970s, a number of small groups advocated radical change and overthrow of the regime. Many were tribally or regionally based, rejecting the term "Saudi" as the name of just one tribe. These groups include the Hijaz Union of the People of the Peninsula, the Revolutionary Najd Party, the Union of the People of the Arabian Peninsula, and the Popular Front for the Liberation of the Arabian Peninsula. Most of these groups were supported by Egypt and Syria, and were expelled by Saudi security forces once Saudi relations with their sponsors improved. One group called the Committee for the Defense of the Rights of the Saudi People is still said to operate in exile in Western Europe. Another, Voice of the Vanguard was established in 1973 espousing liberal democratic values and is financed mainly by some of the approximately 13,000 Saudi students studying in the U.S.

The Grand Mosque Takeover. The most visible demonstration of opposition to the government to date was the

Grand Mosque takeover in Mecca. On November 20, 1979 (the first day of the 15th Islamic century) a group of well-armed gunmen, variously estimated to have numbered a few hundred to several thousand, seized the Grand Mosque, withstanding seige by government troops for almost two weeks. The course of the battle itself was long and painful. An initial police team was driven back by sniper fire. The ulama hesitated for several days before granting the government forces permission to fire within the mosque. The Saudi military, unable to deal with the guerrilla tactics of the gunmen, reportedly called first upon the Jordanians, and then the French for help. (The government denied allegations of outside help because it is forbidden for non-Muslims to enter Mecca, as the French must have done.)

The incident served to increase Western anxiety about the future of the regime. The Saudi government attributed the takeover to religious fanatics. The government claimed that the leader of the revolt had demanded that the pilgrims acknowledge him as the Mahdi, a kinsman of the Prophet who, in Muslim popular culture, reappears periodically to lead the community of believers back to the true way of the Prophet.

Although the government has consistently claimed the revolt was the work of fanatics, there are indications that religious, tribal, and political motivations played a role. Certain tribes received prominent mention. The so-called Mahdi, Muhammad bin Abdallah al-Qahtani came from the Asir, an independent principality annexed by Ibn Saud in 1925. The leader of the insurgents was said to be an ex-National Guardsman, Juhaiman bin Saif al-Oteiba, a brother-in-law of the man proclaimed Mahdi. Juhaiman accused the Saudi regime of hypocrisy and corruption, stating that the Saudi oil production policy (then at 10 mbd) was bankrupting future generations for the sake of dissolute princes and a decadent West. The regime, while claiming to uphold Islamic values, was destroying them by encouraging industrialization and women's education, he said.

Juhaiman and a group of nearly 100 followers were arrested briefly in 1978 after circulating pamphlets calling for the overthrow of the royal family. Four years earlier, while a theology student at the ultra-conservative Islamic University in Medina, he founded a group called the Salafiyya, advocating strict adherence to the practices, social customs and institutions of the First generation of Muslims. Most of the Grand Mosque insurgents proved to be like-minded religious conservatives, including many theology students, opposed to the tradition-breaking consequences of the Royal Family's chosen path to development and outraged by corruption and excess within the Royal family itself. Pious resentment was corrupted in some cases by the persistent animosities of sons of tribal leaders defeated by Ibn Saud over fifty years ago.

Signs of discontent with Saudi rule had surfaced prior to the Mosque attack. In September 1979 several junior army officers suspected of belonging to a loose grouping called the "Movement" were arrested by the authorities. The Movement is thought to include elements of several Bedouin tribes, a few leftist groups, small secret cells of disaffected Army and National Guard personnel, intelligence officers, university students and immigrant workers. Movement members distributed anti-regime literature and created minor disturbances in Phahrau, central Najd, Tabuk and Medina on several occasions in 1978 and 1979. According to some reports, Saudi police arrested some 1,200 suspected Movement members in Mecca and Medina on November 10, 1979. A peaceful protest involving several hundred men, women and children followed at the Grand Mosque, where local police engaged in protracted clashes with the demonstrators.

While it is impossible to accurately estimate the number of Saudis who supported or sympathized with the Grand Mosque rebels, the Saudi government took the threat seriously enough to take nation-wide security measures during the incident and to initiate reforms in its wake. In addition to sealing off Mecca and surrounding the Mosque itself, the government ordered troops into the streets of the major cities, cut all domestic and foreign communications links and urgently apprised the American Embassy of the situation.

Since the Grant Mosque incident, the Saudi government has moved to reduce corruption and to promulgate a Basic Law based on the Quran and the Sunna. The military has been revamped with American assistance, and the government asked the Germans and French for assistance in developing an effective counter-terrorist commando unit.

Shiite Opposition. The Shiite population of the Kingdom, totaling 440,000, is highly concentrated in the Eastern Provinces. Many of the workers in ARAMCO are Shiites, attracted by the high wages and lack of the discrimination to which they are often subject in other economic sectors. There have been a number of reports of Shiite unrest, although it is likely that some of these were part of an Iranian "disinformation" campaign, aimed at destabilizing the government. At the end of November

1979, there were disturbances in Jeddah and around the Dhahran oil fields; some report that the National Guard fired into crowds shouting pro-Khomeini and anti-American slogans. On the first anniversary of Khomeini's return to Iran (February 1, 1980), there were reports that the city of Qatif (98 percent Shiite) was sealed off and that the National Guard killed several demonstrators, resulting in riots. There were also reports of pipeline sabotage in the Eastern oil fields.

Palestinians. Palestinians are not considered a serious threat to the regime. They comprise a smaller percentage of the population (5 percent) than in other peninsula states, and the government holds the PLO responsible for Palestinian behavior. There have been several waves of Palestinian influxes into the Kingdom: 1948, 1952, 1956, and the largest in 1967. Al-Fatah maintains an office in Saudi Arabia to help with visas, social problems and government contacts. Every Palestinian working there donates five percent of his or her income to Palestinian organizations, with the Saudi government assisting in collection.

1.7 POLITICAL ECONOMY. There is probably no more laissez-faire economy anywhere than in Saudi Arabia. This stems in large measure from the Saudis conception of their Islamic heritage. Islam does not consider the material world to be evil. Private property in this view is specifically protected in Islam, with the provision that along with it goes the responsibility to share with the poor. Charity in Islam is not merely a humanitarian good; it is a moral obligation of the rich and a moral right of the poor. Thus, the moral basis for equitable distribution of wealth in Islamic society is based on private property rather than on the collectivist notions of socialist doctrine.

Saudi Islamic capitalism goes one step further. The Hanbali school of Islamic jurisprudence which the Saudis follow is the most liberal of the four orthodox schools on the subject of commerce. Thus, while stealing is reprehensible and the Islamic punishment of cutting off the right hand of a convicted thief is occasionally practiced, in business one can rightfully charge what the market will bear.

The Private Sector. With a market economy philosophy, it is ironic that less than 10 percent of the Saudi economy falls within the private sector. This was not always so, and most of the present Saudi leadership can remember the days before oil when the government depended for most of its revenue on taxes and fees collected during the annual Hajj. In the 1930s, the Great Depression and the rising political turmoil that presaged World War II so curtailed the Hajj that the government was on the edge of bankruptcy.

The Hajj is still the greatest single commercial season in the Kingdom. An estimated one-third of annual retail commerce takes place during the four to six weeks of the Hajj season. Most trade-marked items are imported for resale by exclusive agents.

The Public Sector. In 1982 Saudi oil production and oil revenues began to reflect the impact of the world oil glut; for the last quarter of that year oil production averaged 4.6 mbd with revenues of about $16.5 billion. During 1983 production remained low, stabilizing at about 5 mbd by year's end. Oil sales fell from $117.5 billion in 1981 to $78.6 billion in 1982. This past year, with the lowered OPEC price, revenues were probably not much above $50 billion. As of 1984 it appeared that the OPEC benchmark price of $29 per barrel would be maintained and that OPEC and Saudi production would gradually increase. Having pushed for the OPEC price cut of March 1983, after previously standing firm on the $34 compromise of October 1981, the Saudis are calling for no price increases at least through 1985.

Lower oil sales meant that 1982/83 revenues (the Saudi fiscal year began in April) were more than $20 billion short of expectations. While this was eased by the Saudi tendency to underspend budget allocations, a reserve drawdown was necessitated, reaching about $20 billion for the calendar year 1983. The projected fiscal 1983/84 budget calls for a deficit of about $10 billion.

More than any other Gulf state, Saudi Arabia must coordinate oil production and pricing policies. This is because the range of feasible Saudi oil production is so vast that swings in the production level have an impact on international oil prices. This and increases by other producers could result in a very modest increase (or possibly a decline) in total oil revenues – and vice versa.

Manpower Shortages. As Saudi Arabia has moved to industrialize, it has had to rely extensively on foreign manpower resources. The prohibitions imposed on women reduce the size of the labor force; of some 1.5 million Saudi women, only about 50,000 are employed. The result is an acute labor shortage. The vacancy rate (positions that could not be filled by either foreign or domestic workers) is estimated at around 70,000. The government is committed to manpower training programs and hopes eventually to have Saudis managing and operating its industries. However, the small number of available Saudi males and the resistance certain necessary tasks constitute powerful constraints. The inescapable conclusion is that massive dependence on imported manpower will continue into the indefinite future.

Domestic and Foreign Investment. Although the agricultural sector is no longer of real economic significance, it employs some 20 percent of the labor force. A large reclamation project has been undertaken at al-Hasa oasis, dams for irrigation and flood control have been built in Asir province, and a well-drilling program has been carried out in Najd. The government's policy of high support prices for agricultural production is meant to promote self-sufficiency in several basic foods.

The government is committed to promotion of industry. The seaport and industrial complexes at Yanbu on the Red Sea and Jubayl on the Gulf are the most ambitious projects to date. Each site will serve as a major naval base and Jubayl will be the center of the petrochemical industry. The scope of this development led to creation of a special royal commission to oversee implementation. In undertaking an ambitious policy of industrialization, the Saudis face severe constraints in manpower.

Before the lowered oil earnings of the past two years, Saudi revenues could not be absorbed domestically. To avoid rampant inflation, "excess funds" were invested abroad. It can be assumed that there will again be surplus funds in the future, but of smaller magnitude. Generous overseas aid programs to Arab and other Muslim countries and equity investments in the Muslim world have absorbed some of the surplus. The lion's share of the surplus flowed to western money markets, especially dollar investments, and will continue to do so.

Education and Social Change. The first non-Quranic school in Saudi Arabia was established in Taif in 1940 by Princess Iffat, the wife of the then Prince Faisal. It was originally set up as a private academy for Faisal's sons, the Sudairi cousins (kin to the present King Fahd) and the sons of prominent Hijazi families. As the school's blend of traditional and secular education became accepted, the school was moved to Jeddah, and expanded. The revolution in Saudi education can be seen in the numbers. In 1948 there were only 20,000 students (at all levels of schooling) in Saudi Arabia – all of them male; by 1970 the number had grown to 590,000 and by 1980 it had reached 1.5 million, including more than a half million female students. Over 100,000 students, about one-third of them women, are currently receiving some form of post-secondary training, while adult education classes enroll another 150,00 Saudis. Women students comprise about a quarter of the 50,000 Saudi university students, but only ten percent of the approximately 15,000 Saudis studying abroad. Nearly 70 percent of the Saudis doing their undergraduate or graduate work abroad study in the United States. Another 20 percent study in the Arab countries, most of them in Egypt, 9 percent study in Europe and 1 percent elsewhere in the world. Engineering students account for 33 percent of the total number studying in the United States and students in the social sciences another 25 percent. Only in the fields of medicine, where Saudi students are divided about equally among Egypt, Europe, and the United States and in law, where Egypt hosts twice as many students as the United States, is the United States not the dominant supplier of foreign education to Saudis.

Saudi Arabia is rapidly developing its own capacity to provide higher education to its citizens. Three full-fledged universities are now open and expanding, in addition to the specialized Petroleum Minerals University and two Islamic Universities concentrating on religious studies. The Saudi annual expenditure on education exceeds $5 million.

Women's Education. Because the prospect of education for girls provoked strenuous resistance, Princess Iffat and Princess Faisal, with the backing of King Saud, opened a girls' school in Jeddah in 1956 camouflaged as an orphanage. They claimed inspiration from the Quranic command to care for orphaned children. A year later, Princess Iffat claimed the school was aimed at producing better mothers and homemakers through Islamic instruction based on modern educational theories.

At the time, the present King Fahd, minister of education for King Saud, was heading a massive expansion of state schooling; some of the ideas of the Taif Model School were incoporated into a national syllabus. King Saud established a college for his daughters within the palace, favoring Princess Iffat's ideas. In 1960, a national committee containing members of the ulama was established to oversee the introduction of female education throughout the Kingdom. In addition, Princess Iffat founded a teacher training college in Riyadh. In less than a decade, Princess Iffat managed to enroll over a quarter million girls and women in Saudi schools.

The fact that Saudi tradition dictates that women's social activities be segregated from men encourages rather than prevents the formation of women's cooperative groups. These women's collectives are today among the most active private associations in Saudi life. Princess Iffat's own Saudi Renaissance Movement (SRM) provides free classes in Riyadh to combat adult female illiteracy, runs clinics and dispensaries with classes in hygiene and child care, and organizes courses in foreign languages and typing. All of these activities are funded by the members of the collective, working in cooperation with the Ministry of Labor and Social Affairs. The SRM and other women's action groups that have sprung up in Riyadh and other Saudi towns offer an alternative to traditional family-centered relationships. The SRM and its sister groups provide a context where a Saudi woman can be more than just an accessory in her husband's home. Working exclusively with other women, she can shape an independent identity for herself.

1.8 FACTORS FOR STABILITY AND INSTABILITY. Instability arises when political, social, and economic institutions of a country fail to meet society's expectations. In Saudi Arabia expectations are soaring. This is in part a result of mass education and communications which have thrust an isolated desert kingdom into the center of Middle Eastern and world politics. It is also a function of massive oil revenues which have made yesterday's luxuries today's necessities.

In the face of rising expectations, the strongest bulwark for stability in Saudi Arabia is the society. Though changing, the family as an institution is still sufficiently strong to provide identity, direction, and fulfillment in a social sense. The strong, conservative Islamic values which permeate the society have given a moral direction that has been lacking in other Middle East countries, a lack which has contributed to the resurgence of Islamic fundamentalism in countries such as Iran and Egypt.

At the same time, Islam is a potentially destabilizing force. The 1979 assault on the Great Mosque in Mecca and the Shiite riots of 1979 and 1980, though not necessarily symptomatic of any overriding Saudi political disaffections, called attention to the possibility of

Islamic militance becoming a means of expressing opposition to the regime. Saudi Shiites, influenced by anti-Saudi invective from Iran, could pose a threat to the oil-rich Eastern Province, but could not threaten the regime. There is potential, however, for young Saudi Sunnis to embrace militant Wahhabism and turn against the regime for abandoning Islamic principles. Little evidence of such a tendency currently exists.

Economic institutions are strong. Where inequity of opportunity would create resentment and disaffection in other countries, Saudi Arabia has so much money that a resourceful citizen can develop almost unlimited business opportunities. Inflation could become a catalyst for disaffection, particularly among salaried workers, but strong family ties and weak conflict of interest constraints mean that most salaried workers can share in the wealth through family business ties.

The Saudi regime holds two claims to legitimacy that give it a more solid base than many Arab countries. First, the regime lays claim to the religious legitimacy of the two-centuries-old Wahhabi movement, which it has largely co-opted. The head of the judiciary is usually from the family of Abd al-Wahhab. This co-optation in the short term offers added stability to the regime; in the longer term in the face of militant religious fanaticism, it could serve to undermine the legitimacy of both the religious and governmental establishments. Second, Saudi Arabia has never been directly governed by a colonial or occupying power. Only the Hijaz was under more than nominal hegemony of the Ottoman Empire. Until the development of the oil industry, the entire country was largely ignored by the western powers, hence, Saudis history of recent foreign domination. This, together with Saudi Arabia's very real economic clout, gives Saudis and the Saudi regime a self-assurance in the realm of world politics that is often lacking in Third World countries. On the other hand, Saudi Arabia, while not, like many Arab countries, a creation of the colonial powers, is nonetheless a recent creation. The Kingdom is ruled and will be ruled for some time to come by only the sons of its founder, Ibn Saud. The propriety of Ibn Saud's family rule is by no means universally accepted in the country. It is likely to appear increasingly implausible and, perhaps, unacceptable to rising generations.

Rapid social and economic change provide potential for disaffection. At least two areas merit attention in the coming years: the leadership potential of the current regime and the degree to which a growing desire of younger, educated Saudis for greater public participation in the political process can be met.

2
RECENT DEVELOPMENTS: 1975 – 1984

2.1 INTERNAL DEVELOPMENTS – POLITICAL. The year 1975 saw the end of an era in Saudi Arabia. In March King Faisal was assassinated by an emotionally unbalanced nephew. He was succeeded by a half-brother, King Khalid bin Abd al-Aziz, who had been Crown Prince since 1964. Because Khalid was physically unwell he served as a kind of chairman of the board, making final decisions but leaving day-to-day business in the hands of Crown Prince Fahd ibn Abd al-Aziz. In June 1982 Khalid died of a heart attack and Fahd became King in a smooth transition. At the same time, Abdallah was confirmed as the new Crown Prince and First Deputy Premier while Sultan became Second Deputy Premier and second in the line of royal succession. The rapid and untroubled transition put to rest doubts about whether the Sudairi faction of Fahd and his full brothers would try to contest Abdallah's right to succession on Fahd's death.

Fahd's accession raised expectations, among young technocrats and princes as well as among foreigners, that the new king would institute vigorous reforms to make the system more efficient and more open. These expectations have been disappointed, largely because they mistakenly assumed Fahd's basic guiding principles to be reformist rather than royalist. Moreover, while the King would like to streamline the Saudi government and make it a more effective instrument for carrying out policy, this reflects his desire to promote and consolidate royal power, not a belief that more initiative and authority should be given to technocrats and junior princes. Although the King is reputed to want an administrative overhaul to increase the bureaucracy's efficiency, he has done little along these lines.

In part this reflects failure to persuade Abdallah to relinquish his command of the National Guard, a move that Fahd sees as necessary before embarking on major governmental reorganization. During the period of succession following Faisal's death, one small incident highlights the rivalry between Fahd and Abdallah. Once the King and

Crown Prince were chosen, the princes and tribal leaders were expected to swear an oath of loyalty (baya) to the new heir apparent. All of the princes did this in person, with the exception of Abdallah, who sent a telegram. Khalid demanded and ultimately received the oath of fealty to Fahd in person.

Fahd favors establishment of a consultative council (Majlis al-Shura), but this appears to have been shelved indefinitely in deference to the religious establishment which would oppose dilution of their power. On the positive side, despite friction between Fahd and Abdallah, they have worked together smoothly, with the latter gaining useful experience for the day he succeeds Fahd. While differences of opinion exist between them, rumors of violent antagonism are exaggerated. The government functions well and, Sudairi ambitions notwithstanding, it is unlikely that Sultan would challenge Abdallah's right to the throne.

2.2 ECONOMIC. While completion of infrastructure projects, especially outside the major urban centers, continues to absorb significant funding, there has been a major shift of emphasis in the Third Plan, launched in 1980/81. More than a third of the development budget will be spent to expand and diversify "productive" sectors, meaning mostly industry. This reflects efforts to expand the private sector, which by 1981/82 had increased its share of the GDP to about 35 percent. While trade and commerce continue to be the main form of private sector activity, generous government subsidies are encouraging private investment in construction and other industries, in banking and in agriculture, where attempts to promote self-sufficiency in basic foodstuffs such as wheat are being promoted with subsidies equal to 50 percent of input costs. The government's goal is to bring about eventual private ownership (by individuals or corporations) of all sectors of the economy except petroleum extraction.

The allocation of 1983/84 funds reflects the Third Plan's strong emphasis on human resource development (education and manpower training), with the outlay representing the largest share of non-military spending apart from administrative expenditures. The intent of this development is to reduce heavy dependence upon foreign manpower. However, the small size of the Saudi workforce and continued cultural aversion to certain kinds of jobs makes progress toward this goal dubious. Women are confined to jobs in which they can be segregated – medicine and education as well as some retail trade and banking.

2.3 REVENUE REDUCTION. Reduced revenues due to the continuing oil glut have caused no severe economic dislocation or significant social or political stress. Some projects have been cut and others stretched out over longer periods of time than originally envisaged. In addition, the government has slowed payments to contractors, Saudi and foreign. While this has caused some disgruntlement among Saudi businessmen, the impact should not be severe, since the government remains committed to promoting the indigenous private sector. Saudi per capita income is still among the highest in the world and economic activity in the country remains robust, especially in the construction, retail trade and agricultural sectors. Key domestic and foreign expenditure commitments continue to be honored, including national defense, various welfare and subsidy payments to Saudi citizens and foreign aid disbursements to states of prime strategic or political concern to Saudi Arabia. Moreover, despite the shift from overall rapid GDP growth to decline, the non-oil component of the GDP has increased to slightly less than half the total, promoting a key government goal of reduced dependence on oil income. A somewhat reduced pace of development may have social and political benefits. Many Saudis have felt that the previous level of expenditure engendered changes which were too rapid and massive for the Kingdom to absorb and still maintain its conservative Islamic values.

3
EXTERNAL DEVELOPMENT

3.1 SAUDI STRATEGY. For years, Saudi Arabia tried to stay out of Arab politics. Its leaders were convinced that attendance at intra-Arab conclaves would subject them either to Nasserist and other leftist tirades or to requests for money. This self-imposed low profile began to change in the early 1970s. With the death of Nasser, followed by the psychological Arab victory in the 1973 Arab-Israeli War, Saudi Arabia saw an opportunity for Arab moderates to seize the initiative and obtain an acceptable settlement from Israel. The Saudi oil weapon was to be a major factor in the new policy.

3.2 THE ARAB/ISRAELI PROBLEM. Following the Sinai II agreement of 1974, which divided Egypt and Syria, the Saudis endeavored, in 1976 at the Riyadh summit, to restore Arab unity and promote a peace embracing Palestinian rights to self-determination. Sadat's trip to Jerusalem in 1977 and the Camp David Accords and Egyptian-Israeli Treaty in the following two years sidetracked this effort. The Saudis saw Camp David not as leading to a comprehensive settlement but as generating further instability in the Arab world and, therefore, increased threat to themselves. This prompted then Crown Prince Fahd, in an uncharacteristically forward Saudi initiative, to launch an eight-point peace plan – the so-called "Fahd Plan" – in summer 1981. It accepted at least by implication Israel's existence within secure borders. Presented to the Arab League states at the November 1981 summit in Morocco, it was defeated by Syrian opposition. In modified form (with significant input from Yasser Arafat), it was approved a year later, a few days after the Reagan Plan which called for a federation between the West Bank and Jordan. Despite the considerable gap between the terms of the two plans, the Saudis see them as complementary efforts to promote a peace settlement. They gave diplomatic support to the abortive effort to bring about an agreement between Jordan and the PLO in early 1983. However, the Saudis believe that U.S. failure to press the Reagan Plan upon Israel has caused it to become a dead letter.

3.3 THE ISLAMIC WORLD. Saudi Arabia feels a special responsibility toward the Islamic world as keeper of two of Islam's three holiest shrines, Mecca and Medina (the third is Jerusalem). This colors its foreign policy perspective. The late King Saud in the 1950s created the Islamic World League primarily to oppose Nasserism, which he thought endangered Islam. King Faisal was the prime mover in the creation of the Islamic Foreign Ministers Conference. Under Kings Khalid and Fahd, Saudi concern with Islamic world affairs has continued.

In recent years, certain forces in the Islamic world have come to be seen as a threat by Saudi leaders. From the Saudi perspective, the new Islamic fundamentalism is not only a theological threat – as strict Wahhabis, they see it as a theological aberration – but also as political threat. Its champions care more for the primacy of their narrow beliefs than for the unity of the Islamic world against the potent dangers of atheistic communism and western secularism. Islamic fundamentalists, such as those in Iran or the assassins of President Sadat, by setting Muslim against Muslim, are seen in Saudi Arabia as a threat to the entire Islamic world.

The attack on the mosque in Mecca by Muslim extremists gave the current Saudi leadership its first direct experience with the movement. The incident not only shook the royal family, but sensitized the ruling circle to the potential dangers of outraged Muslim sentiment. Consequently, there has been greater attention paid to public sentiment at all levels. Princes hold more frequent audiences in various parts of the kingdom, giving citizens an opportunity to express their needs directly, the ruling authorities keep their finger on the pulse of the country, and more apparent heed is taken of the views of the religious establishment. This response has a mild restraining influence on Saudi domestic and foreign policies. Such practices are likely to continue – and even be intensified in times of trouble – into the forseeable future.

3.4 RELATIONS WITH SOUTH ARABIA. Saudi Arabia has always guarded its preeminence in the Arabian Peninsula. It prefers that countries such as Oman and the Yemens be weak buffer states, without destabilizing radical ideologies. When Nasser's secular pan-Arabism threatened to infect North Yemen in the 1960s, Saudi Arabia intervened on the royalist side. Similarly, they gave financial and military assistance to Oman at the time of the rebellion in the Dhofar region. The Saudis look askance at Soviet assistance to both North and South Yemen. Increased assistance from Saudi Arabia and the GCC has considerably moderated the stance of both countries.

In addition to security considerations, there are an estimated one million workers from the North Yemen resident in Saudi Arabia. Many of these have kinship ties to tribes across the border, and until the 1970s emigrated freely into the Kingdom. There are now greater restrictions, although there has been considerable forging of passports and other evidence of Saudi citizenship. Most of the Yemeni workers live in poverty compared to Saudi citizens, remitting three-fourths of their earnings to their home country, where the 1978 per capita income was $420. Saudi Arabia has in the past feared that South Yemeni infiltration into North Yemen would radicalize their guest workers.

3.5 EGYPT. Saudi Arabia has cautiously sought to promote reintegration of Mubarak's Egypt into the Arab world, letting Iraq, Jordan and others take the lead. It played a key part in bringing Egypt back into the Islamic Conference Organization in January 1984. There are a number of reasons why the Saudis would welcome an eventual reintegration of Egypt into the Arab world. Middle Eastern diplomacy is frequently based on personalities; Sadat, perceived as a traitor in the Arab world, is gone, so reintegration is possible. Mubarak is seen as distancing himself from Camp David. He recalled the Egyptian ambassador to Israel following the invasion of Lebanon, and is adamant on the question of Jerusalem. Mubarak visited Saudi Arabia following Khalid's death in 1982. Egypt has provided arms and perhaps a small number of men to Iraq in its fight against Iran. Last, there are still a number of Egyptian workers in Saudi Arabia, although fewer than prior to Camp David. Despite Egypt's increased acceptance in the Arab fold, there are limits to which the Saudis or any other Arabs will go so long as Egypt remains firm to its treaty obligations to Israel. From the Saudi perspective, full Egyptian rapprochement depends on progress toward a comprehensive Arab-Israeli peace. In addition, Saudi Arabia has historically feared a strong Egypt. Egyptians launched the only two successful invasions of the peninsula – that of Muhammad Ali in 1806 and that of Nasser in support of a revolution in North Yemen, from 1962 to 1967.

3.6 RELATIONS WITH JORDAN, IRAQ AND SYRIA. Prior to the mid-1960s, there was considerable dynastic rivalry with the Hashemite Kingdom in Jordan. That dynasty claimed descent from the Prophet, and had been resident in the Hijaz prior to World War I. The Saudis and Hashemites were rivals for western support; the Saudis had American advisors, while the Hashemites had British advisors. Until the overthrow of the Hashemite dynasty in Iraq in 1958, the Saudis were hostile towards both Jordan and Iraq. This explains why they did not join the Baghdad Pact, the anti-Communist alliance of Iraq, Iran, Turkey, and Pakistan engineered by John Foster Dulles in the 1950s, which later became the CENTO Pact. Relations between the two warmed in the 1960s, the Saudis gave Jordan large sums for reconstruction and development.

The Saudis feared the pan-Arab, secularist appeal of the Baathist ideology promoted by Iraq and Syria during the 1960s. Along with Nasser, these states gave financial support to the miniscule opposition groups which arose in the Arabian Peninsula during this period. After 1973, relations with Iraq improved, partly due to the coordination within OPEC, although Iraq criticized the Saudi oil pricing policy. Syria is a more complex situation. There have always been some links between the two governments. For example, Rifaat al-Assad (head of Syrian intelligence and most likely the next Syrian President) married his daughter to the Crown Prince Abdullah. The financial assistance given Syria as a "confrontation state" against Israel has continued despite Syrian support of Iran in the Gulf War. Within the GCC, Saudi Arabia is the only state not to have broken with Syria over its policies in Lebanon and the Gulf. However, continued assistance to Syria should not be seen as a sign of weakness. The Saudis have other ways of indicating their displeasure, such as slowing down payments. In addition, the present Syrian rulers are Alawites, considered almost heretics to Sunni Islam. There is some evidence that the Saudis have in the past funneled assistance to the anti-regime Muslim Brotherhood in Syria, and this could easily be resumed.

3.7 ISRAEL. Saudi Arabia has no diplomatic relations with Israel, but for years has declared that it is not a confrontation state. Such a position was acceptable to Israel until it realized that Saudi oil was the one Arab weapon that could ultimately undermine Israel's vital U.S. support. Although this apprehension has been dissipated by the realities of oil and politics, Israel has nonetheless done its best in recent years to have Saudi Arabia perceived as a confrontation state. Israeli statements that Saudi Arabia would be attacked in a future conflict, together with the Israeli raid of 1981 on Iraq's nuclear reactor and other provocative Israeli overflights of Saudi territory, have convinced the Saudis that Israel is a direct military threat to them. Moreover, Saudi Arabia perceives Israel as a cancer in the midst of the Islamic world and the principal factor accounting for the radicalization of the Arab states. Saudi Arabia considers Israel's occupation of Islam's third holiest site, the Aqsa Mosque in Jerusalem, an affront to all Muslims. Saudis believe that the only way to solve the problem is to guarantee Palestinian rights (including territorial rights) and return Islamic holy places in Jerusalem to Muslim (i.e., Arab) control. Since they believe that Israel will never accede to such terms voluntarily, their main thrust has been for moderate Arabs in a united front to convince the United States that its best interests lie in forcing Israel into a just peace with the Arabs.

3.8 THE PLO. It has been hinted broadly in the west that Saudi support of the PLO is based on fear of terrorist reprisals. While support to the PLO is an important form of purchasing protection (though in the present fractured state of the PLO this is less urgent), the Saudis support the Palestinian cause on moral and political grounds even more than for reasons of expediency. Moreover, their support is selective. They have never supported the radical PLO groups which they believe to be atheistic. Yasser Arafat, on the other hand, not only leads the moderate Fatah, but was once a follower of Hassan al-Banna, the Egyptian founder of the arch-conservative Muslim Brotherhood. Arafat's cooperation in getting the second Fahd Plan accepted, his willingness to draw closer to King Hussein and President Mubarak, and to find a negotiated settlement has made Fatah even more palatable to the Saudis. Thus, Fatah has been and will continue to be a recipient of Saudi generosity and support. The internecine fighting in Lebanon between the Arafat faction and the Syrian-backed militants led by Abu Musa has fortified Saudi backing for Arafat and strengthened Saudi anger against Syria. High-handed Syrian dismissal of Saudi mediation efforts among the warring Palestinians has caused a minor breach with the Syrians (already in bad odor for supporting Iran against Iraq), which is likely to manifest itself in the forums of inter-Arab politics.

3.9 LEBANON. Prior to the outbreak of the civil war in 1975, the Saudis had ties with two Lebanese groups. There was a large expatriate Maronite Christian community in the Kingdom, some of whom have risen to high positions within the Saudi government as trusted financial advisors. There were also ties to Said Saladin and the conservative Sunni Muslim merchants. Neither the Shiites in the South nor the Druze of Kamal Jumblatt had such ties.

Since the outbreak of the Lebanese Civil War, the Saudis have devoted considerable efforts to trying to bring peace, both bilaterally with Lebanon and Syria and through multilateral Arab peacekeeping efforts. The Israeli invasion of Lebanon in 1982 linked the Lebanese situation to the broader Arab-Israeli problem. In seeking a solution, Saudi Arabia was drawn in close association with American diplomacy into what was ultimately to become the hopeless cause of inducing both Israelis and Syrians to withdraw. This phase of the problem ended with withdrawal of U.S. marines from Beirut in early 1984. The Saudis place blame for the failure squarely on the United States, claiming the May 17, 1983 Israeli-Lebanese accord was far too accommodating to Israel. In addition, it totally undercut Saudi efforts to persuade Syria to cooperate in a joint withdrawal. Saudi cooperation with U.S. diplomacy in Lebanon would probably have exposed them to far more vitriolic attacks from Arab radicals had not Syria itself broken Arab ranks by supporting Iran in its war with Iraq, and had not Baghdad become so indebted to the Saudis for financial and other support. Saudi efforts toward a Lebanese solution – such as they are – reflect a shift away from cooperation with American initiatives (discredited in Saudi eyes) toward an Arab approach.

3.10 WITH NON-ARAB MUSLIM COUNTRIES With the defection of Egypt, Saudi Arabia found it necessary to seek other Muslim military allies. There has been some success with Pakistan. Saudi Arabia has given considerable military and economic assistance to Pakistan; in exchange, Zia ul-Haq has intensified his program of Islamization, despite domestic opposition. In addition, Pakistani troops (Muslim but non-Arabic speaking) supplement the National Guard in its task of protecting the Royal Family. Pakistani economic well-being is also linked to that of Saudi Arabia by virtue of the several hundred thousand Pakistanis working in the Kingdom. Turkey is another Muslim country with increasing military and economic ties to Saudi Arabia, although not as much as Turkish leaders would like.

The Kingdom supported the Islamic National Salvation Party in Turkey prior to the military takeover in 1980; since the reestablishment of government authority in Turkey, Saudi Arbia has supported the government. Saudi Arabia is the only Arab country to give diplomatic support to Turkey against Greece regarding Cyprus. Saudi Arabia has permitted increasing numbers of Turkish guest workers, and has encouraged Turkish firms doing business in the Kingdom.

3.11 THE IRAN-IRAQ WAR. The Saudis view the Iran-Iraq war as the greatest immediate threat to Saudi national security. When Iraq attacked Iran in September 1980, Saudi sympathies were on the side of Iraq, but the Saudis tried hard to avoid becoming directly involved. Their indirect support of Iraq, however, made them vulnerable to Iranian reprisal attack, which led them to lease and later purchase AWACS surveillance aircraft from the United States. The creation of the Gulf Cooperation Council (GCC) by Saudi Arabia and the Arab Gulf states (Kuwait, Bahrain, Qatar, UAE, and Oman) in February 1981 was also in part the result of the perceived threat to Gulf security posed by the war. GCC efforts to coordinate defense measures among its members (i.e. joint military exercises) have increased lately, but with mixed results. That there has been any cooperation at all is an indication of the severity of the threat.

As the war dragged on, the GCC states began to become more directly involved in underwriting the Iraqi war effort through financial support, now over $25 billion. With a growing cash flow problem due to the slackening of oil revenues, the GCC states have had increasing difficulty maintaining these subsidies. The Saudis have urged American cooperation in constructing an Iraqi oil pipeline through Saudi Arabia to the Red Sea to increase Iraqi oil revenues. (Iraq's terminals in the Gulf have been destroyed by Iran, and the pipeline to Syria was closed by the Syrians. Iraq's only export outlet, therefore is a pipeline through Turkey; with a maximum capacity of 1 mbd.) In June 1984 the U.S. Export Import Bank agreed to help finance an Iraqi pipeline to Aqaba, Jordan to be constructed by Bechtel.

In the meantime, Saudi Arabia has also become involved in the war militarily. In the spring of 1984 Iraq, using Entendard aircraft and Exocet air-to-surface missiles purchased from France, began interdicting oil tankers bound for Kharg Island, Iran's major terminal. In retaliation, Iran began using its F-4 Phantom aircraft to bomb tankers on the Arab (mainly Saudi) side of the Gulf.

In June 1984 two Saudi F-15's responded, shooting down an Iranian F-4. It is still too early to determine the full effect or direction of this new phase of the Iran-Iraq war, but for Saudi Arabia the prospect of military involvement has become a reality which the ruling circle still fervently wishes to avoid. In addition to the untested quality of its military, the vulnerability of its oil installations, the political fallout of hostilities with Iran among its Shiite minority and other radical elements – particularly if the Saudi military did not acquit itself well – would be loaded with serious consequences. Thus, the Saudi government will continue to do all it can to stay out of the hostilities and to promote an end to the war.

3.12 THE WEST – THE U.S. The Saudis view the United States as the primary bulwark against the expansion of communism and thus feel a strong mutuality of interest. This bond is strengthened by Saudi respect for U.S. technology. The period of 1975-84 has, therefore, been frustrating for the Saudis. In the mid-1970s, the United States was still in the post-Vietnam mentality of self-evaluation, reassessment, and quasi-isolationism. Thus, communist advances in southern Africa and, more alarmingly, in South Yemen and Ethiopia, appeared to the Saudis to go unheeded by the United States. Saudi concern was heightened by the American response to the Iranian revolution. Only after the Soviet invasion of Afghanistan did the United States, in the Saudi view, begin once again to take on its responsibilities as the protector of the free world. With a swing of the pendulum, however, the Saudis are now concerned that too great a U.S. focus on the Soviet military threat in the Gulf, with attendant pressure for bases or pre-positioning military equipment, could undermine Gulf security since the U.S., in the absence of an Arab-Israeli treaty, is still seen in Arab eyes as abetting Zionist expansionism.

In October 1981, the U.S. Senate, after intense pressure from the Administration and intense opposition from the American Israel lobby, approved the sale of AWACS surveillance aircraft and an enhancement package for the F-15s purchased by (but not yet delivered to) the Saudis in 1978. The approval was crucial for U.S.-Saudi relations as it had become a "litmus test" of U.S. commitment to the Kingdom to meet what the Saudis believed (on the basis of U.S. advice) was their legitimate defense needs. The transfer of Stinger missiles to Saudi Arabia in response to Iranian attacks on Saudi shipping in the spring of 1984 was a boost to U.S.-Saudi relations.

Despite the sale, Saudi Arabia has remained highly ambivalent about its relations with the United States. The Saudis' perception of unwavering U.S. support of Israel and nagging doubts about the U.S. commitment to the defense of the Saudi regime are the main causes of ambivalence. Saudi anxiety over the U.S. commitment to the regime was increased by U.S. passivity to the fall of the Shah 1979. In the present atmosphere of extreme tension due to the Iran-Iraq war, anxiety is likly to continue.

3.13 WESTERN EUROPE AND JAPAN. Saudi Arabia's policies toward western Europe and Japan are based on their inclusion in the free world. In the Saudi view, these countries, even collectively, would not be able to contain communism completely without the participation of the United States; their political support of the Arab cause is important, however, and their role in maintaining the stability of the western economy is crucial. Politically, Saudi policy toward Europe and Japan has aimed at obtaining more support for the Arab cause, including using their influence with the United States. Economically, the Saudis have attempted to increase imports from all these countries in order not to be overly dependent on a single country, particularly the United States. In this regard, trade with South Korea is also important. Militarily, the Saudis would like to buy more weapons from western Europe to lessen its dependence on U.S. arms, but limitations in supply and compatibility of weapons systems create constraints. Nevertheless, France is providing the backbone of the Saudi navy, and in January 1984, the Saudis placed with the French a $4 billion order for an anti-aircraft system.

3.14 THE COMMUNIST WORLD. The Saudis do not distinguish politically between the Soviets, eastern Europe, and China. All are atheist, and no political relations with them exist. This does not prevent trade, particularly with China. The Saudis have been extremely concerned by rising Soviet influence in Ethiopia and South Yemen and by the Soviet invasion of Afghanistan in 1979. These moves accentuate a deeply ingrained encirclement complex developed over centuries of inland desert isolation. They look to the United States to reverse these communist gains, but not to the extent of accepting foreign bases on

Saudi soil. From time to time, high level Saudis hint at resumption of diplomatic relations with the Soviets (suspended since 1938). While occasional exchanges of notes and Foreign Minister Prince Saud's December 1982 visit to Moscow with an Arab delegation have raised U.S. concerns, Saudi fear of a Soviet presence in the Kingdom is likely to preclude diplomatic relations for some time to come.

3.15 THE THIRD WORLD. As has been shown, the Saudis are more concerned by the distinction between God-fearing and godless regimes than between rich and poor or north and south. In order of priority, for example, Saudi aid recipients have been Arab states first, other Islamic states second, and Third World states a distant third. Even then, most aid in the last category goes to states where there is a perceived communist threat.

4
PRESENT SITUATION

4.1 INTERNAL. The Saudis were concerned over the fall of the Shah and whether a similar situation could develop in the Kingdom. Concern was heightened by the Mecca Mosque incident in November 1979 involving religious and tribal zealots who briefly seized the Great Mosque, and by civil disturbances among Shiites in the Eastern Province in early 1980. These incidents, while serious, are not analogous to the grass roots social and political revolution in Iran. They are indicative, however, of the heightened level of social and political tension in the region.

In response to this challenge, the Saudi government has been formulating major reforms, including a clamp-down on corruption and increasing public participation in the political process through a consultative assembly. To date, few of these reforms have been implemented. While Fahd has imposed new restrictions on the behavior of Saudis (including princes) and foreigners, his own lack of standing with the religious establishment and his continued ostentatious life style are apt to be a liability to the monarchy.

In June 1983, King Fahd proposed in a speech to the International Islamic Jurisprudence Council to establish a world academy of Islamic jurisprudence to develop Islamic answers for the modern Muslim world. While it is unlikely that the Muslim world would ever reach a consensus to "reopen the doors of ijtihad (interpretation)," there are both domestic and international implications to the proposal. Domestically, some see this as a move to redress inconsistencies in government policies, undercutting the power of religious leaders giving them a role in shaping new policies. Internationally, the "reopening of ijtihad" is a move to reclaim the leadership of the Islamic world from the diffuse forces of fundamentalism. These are composed mostly of young people, who have been disappointed by the failure of ideologies such as secular Arab socialism and western democracy to provide upward mobility or meaning for their lives. They are turning in disorganized fashion to Sufi orders or small Ikhwan-like sects. The Wahhabis strongly disapprove of Sufism, but wholeheartedly support the orthodox Muslim Brothers.

4.2 EXTERNAL. The Saudis are deeply fearful of Iranian threats. Air attack, subversion, challenges to Saudi oil policy in OPEC, and propaganda assaults on the legitimacy of the Saudi regime and its Islamic credentials are all cause for alarm. In the summer of 1984, these apprehensions motivated the Saudis to invite leading Iranian spokesmen, including Rafsanjani, the Speaker of the Iranian Assembly, to use the opportunity afforded by the Pilgrimmage to hold discussions in Riyadh about Saudi-Iranian relations and other matters (presumably the Iran-Iraq war). Rafsanjani did not reject the proposal outright, indicating a possible shift in Iran's posture. However, it is unlikely that any significant changes in Iran's attitude or policies vis-a-vis the Gulf or the western powers will occur while Khomeini remains in control.

While relying on the United States as its principal military source of support and its ultimate safety net, the Saudis fear too close an embrace of Washington as a political liability – domestic and foreign. U.S. failure to do more to achieve a solution to the other leading source of threat in Saudi eyes – the Arab-Israeli conflict and Palestinian question – disturbs the Saudis. Increasingly they see the United States as unable or unwilling to curb aggressive Israeli behavior or to gain Israeli acceptance of Washington's own positions on the issue of a Middle East peace settlement. At the same time, the Saudis acknowledge that only the U.S. has the potential leverage to move Israel toward a diplomatic solution. Moreover, the Saudis are generally pleased with the strong position of the Reagan administration toward checking the spread of Soviet influence, though they see the threat to their area more in terms of subversion – facilitated by the instability produced by the Arab-Israeli conflict – than as a direct military danger. The U.S.-Saudi relationship remains basically sound but increasingly subject to friction. This may lead to some degree of political distancing on the part of the Saudis. In that connection it should be pointed out that Saudi Arabia tends to compartmentalize its relationship with the United States, so that strained political relations do not necessarily have a substantial negative impact on economic or military relations.

5
FUTURE PROSPECTS

5.1 TIME OF TENSION. Saudi Arabia is experiencing a period of tension unmatched in recent history. The escalation of the Iran-Iraq war to involve Saudi military action with little hope of a peaceful resolution, the continuing strife in Lebanon, the lack of any movement on the Arab-Israeli problem, the oil glut, and the ongoing continuing Soviet threat from Afghanistan to Ethiopia have all serve to heighten the Saudi feeling of encirclement by hostile forces and to underscore the Saudi sense of helplessness. This tension is likely to continue, taking its toll on Saudi domestic and foreign policies alike.

5.2 DOMESTIC POLICY. Saudis do not face an imminent threat to internal security, but the tensions of modernization and regional strife are affecting the equanimity of the population. The regime is and will continue to be sensitive to the increasingly vocal demands of the religious leadership to stem the spread of westernization in the Kingdom. When coupled with the cashflow problems brought on by the oil glut, this is likley to result in a scaling down of development programs over the next few years, including the number of expatriate firms and personnel doing business in Saudi Arabia. However, perceived security threats will ensure a continued high level of Saudi expenditure for defense, though it is likely that American firms will lose more contracts to European competitors.

Nevertheless, the challenges before the regime are formidable. Hundreds of returning college students with new ideas and rising expectations must be assimilated into the society and the economic system, and ultimately must be granted expanded participation in the political process. Traditional governmental checks and balances, oversight and accountability procedures must be continually upgraded to keep pace with ever more sophisticated demands on the government. In short, it will be a time calling for dynamic and inspiring leadership.

5.3 U.S.-SAUDI RELATIONS. It is remarkable how close U.S.-Saudi relations are considering how little either side understands the other. This has largely been so because of mutually perceived interests which both sides believe are best addressed through cooperation – the Soviet threat, regional security, oil market stability, and technology transfer to name a few. The mutual interests remain; however, due to the regional tensions and Saudi anxieties over U.S. commitment to the regime and to a truly even-handed U.S. Middle East policy, relations are likly to be more strained than in previous years.

5.4 RELATIONS WITH THE ARAB STATES. The Arab world is in more disarray than at any time in the last quarter century. Syria has sided with Iran against Iraq, splitting the Arab radical ranks; Egypt, while closer to the Arab fold, has not been totally re-accepted. In this environment, the Saudi role as leader of the moderates is in a somewhat confused state. Little or no progress is being made on an Arab-Israeli peace, the Reagan plan or the Fahd plan, and the Camp David initiative is dormant if not dead. The Saudis are likely to try to regroup, hoping for some sort of peace initiative after the U.S. elections of 1984. As with so many of their problems, however, they have relatively little ability to dictate an outcome to their liking and will probably continue to be frustrated over what they see as a lack of real progress toward the realization of Palestinian rights.

5.5 ISLAMIC WORLD. Saudi Arabia has good relations with all Islamic states with the exception of Iran. The threat of militant Islamic fundamentalism will continue to be major concern to the Saudi regime.

5.6 TOWARD A NEW CONSENSUS. Fortunately, the government is aware of the problems confronting it, but creating consensus to deal with them has often been agonizingly slow. In recent years, the leadership appears to have entered a dangerous period of malaise, with indecisiveness impeding decision in a multitude of complex matters. However, younger and highly trained Saudis, both in the royal family and out, are motivated and eager to help serve their country. With adequate use of this new talent base and a renewed sense of purpose, the challenge can be met. For the survival of the regime, there is no other alternative.

III. ECONOMIC ANALYSIS

1
SUMMARY CONCLUSIONS

1.1 GDP GROWTH. After a period of rapid GDP (Gross Domestic Product) growth, fuelled by rapidly increasing oil revenues, GDP growth became negative in 1982 and 1983 as oil income dropped sharply. Improved oil market conditions made a modest recovery, making low but stable GDP growth likely as early as this year (1984). However, the days of unlimited growth and massive government spending on "megaprojects" are over for good.

1.2 SECTORAL BREAKDOWN OF GDP. The oil and gas sector continues to dominate the Saudi economy. Construction, previously of considerable significance, is declining in importance as a result of the completion of many projects and the scaling down of development in light of lower revenues. The service sector (including finance) continues to grow steadily. The manufacturing and agricultural sectors will remain small in terms of their contribution to the GDP.

1.3 ECONOMIC PLANNING. Saudi Arabia has a long history of successful medium-term economic planning. Recent shifts in priorities point to the growing importance attached to manpower development, integration in the Gulf Cooperation Council, and matching expenditure with government revenues (i.e., fiscal conservatism). The long-standing goals of increasing private sector participation in economic development and diversifying the economy remain paramount.

1.4 PUBLIC POLICY. The new (1984/85) Saudi budget projects a deficit of SR 45.9 billion ($13.09 billion), an indication that the government is concerned about the slowdown of economic activity. At the same time, the maintenance of expenditure at the 1983/84 nominal level indicates that the government is making an effort to avoid long-term commitments in the face of uncertain oil revenues.

1.5 THE OIL SECTOR. Saudi Arabia enjoys the largest proven oil reserves of any country in the world. Production rates (now at 5 mbd) have varied considerably. Saudi Arabia is unique among GCC states in that it has a very wide range of physically and financially feasible production levels. The objectives of Saudi Arabia's oil production and pricing policies are: orderly conditions in the oil market, a high enough level of production to meet long-term needs, and maximization of revenue from oil and financial investments.

1.6 THE AGRICULTURAL SECTOR. The development of the agricultural sector is constrained by such considerations as extreme water scarcity, soil infertility, adverse climatic conditions, expensive labor, and marketing difficulties. Nonetheless, the government is strongly committed to developing the agricultural sector, partly because it wishes to improve the standard of living of rural inhabitants and partly because it is fearful of a food boycott.

1.7 MANUFACTURING SECTOR. Non-hydrocarbon manufacturing industries are of negligible importance in Saudi Arabia. The Saudis are anxious to develop their manufacturing sector as a means of insuring a fair degree of economic diversification, resource development, and regional balance. The emphasis has been on involving the Saudi private sector in industrial investment through generous incentives amd subsidies, and the promotion of joint ventures.

1.8 MANPOWER. Like most GCC countries, Saudi Arabia is subject to severe manpower constraints. The lack of interest in certain employment skills on the part of the indigenous population, and the reluctance to employ women, have intensified the problem. The number of foreign (notably Asian) workers in Saudi Arabia has grown rapidly in recent years, to the point of presenting serious social and political problems. The Saudi have begun to discourage the employment of foreigners and stress training programs in all fields for their native population.

1.9 THE FINANCIAL SECTOR. The Saudi Arabian Monetary Agency (SAMA) has begun playing a more forceful role in controlling the Kingdom's money supply and financial sector. Money changers have been subjected to stricter regulation, and banks to limitations on borrowing as a percentage of their capital. At the same time, SAMA has sought to impose tighter controls over riyal syndications. On the whole, the financial sector in Saudi Arabia has fared reasonably well, with commercial bank credit to the private sector continuing to grow in 1982/83, albeit at a reduced rate. Saudi Arabian businessmen have been active in the development of Islamic banking in Saudi Arabia and elsewhere.

1.10 BALANCE OF PAYMENTS. Saudi exports are dominated by sales of crude. These have fluctuated considerably in recent years, peaking in 1982, declining sharply in 1983, and then recovering in 1984. Imports maintained steady growth until 1983, when decline reflected the lower level of economic activity as a result of lower oil revenues. The balance of trade surplus was eliminated in 1983, swinging into deficit and back into surplus in the course of the year. The balance of services and transfers has traditionally been in deficit. The current account has acted erratically; the usual surplus was eliminated in 1983. SAMA holds substantial foreign assets, although these shrank in 1983 when they were drawn down to meet expenses. Saudi Arabia is a major donor of aid, which it regards as an instrument of foreign policy. It has dispensed aid: (1) bilaterally, (2) through its donor agency, the Saudi Development Fund and (3) through multilateral agencies.

2
MACRO-ECONOMIC ANALYSIS

2.1 RECENT DEVELOPMENTS: STRUCTURAL CHANGES (1967 – 1978). During the twelve-year period between 1967 and 1978, the Saudi Arabian economy underwent many structural changes. Some of these changes were the consequence of government policies, some were inevitable given the large sectoral imbalance in the natural resources of the country, and some were caused by factors exogenous to the domestic economy and beyond the direct control of public officials.

Structural changes caused by the first two factors can be described best by examining the sectoral distribution of the GDP. Three non-oil sectors, agriculture, business services, and construction, present particularly interesting cases in point. Even before the oil-price boom of 1973/74, the contribution of the agricultural sector (which includes agriculture, forestry, and fishing) to the GDP was declining steadily. It declined from around 6.5 percent in 1966/67* to less than 4 percent in 1972/73 and to around 3.2 percent in 1977/78. Given the disadvantage of this sector with respect to the country's natural resources, the growth in agriculture could not keep pace with the growth in the rest of the economy. However, this does not mean that the agriculture sector was stagnant during this period. It grew at an annual rate of around 3.5 percent between 1966/67 and 1972/73, and at around 4.7 percent per year between 1973/74 and 1977/78.

Construction and business services are the two major non-oil sectors which benefited most from the oil boom of 1973/74. The share of the construction sector in the

---

* Saudi Arabia national accounts are based on a fiscal year which uses the lunar Hijra calendar year. Hijra years are approximately eleven days shorter than Gregorian calendar years.

total GDP increased from 6 percent in 1966/67 to 11 percent in 1977/78. The share of the business sector increased from 6 percent to 8.3 percent during the same period.

2.2 THE PETROLEUM SECTOR (1969 – 1978). It should be noted that all percentage shares are estimated at constant 1969/70 prices. Given the very sharp increase in oil prices in 1973/74, these shares would be considerably lower if estimated, for example, at constant 1974/75 prices. This point will be demonstrated briefly in an examination of the share of the petroleum sector.

At constant 1969/70 prices, the petroleum sector (crude oil mining and petroleum refining) contributed about 51 percent of the GDP in 1966/67. This share increased steadily until it peaked at around 62 percent in 1973/74, and then started to decline, reaching about 51 percent in 1977/78. At constant 1974/75 prices, the petroleum sector looks much more important, accounting for 73 to 81 percent of the GDP. The drop in the contribution of the oil sector in 1974/75 was due partially to a drop in oil production which, in turn, was due to dwindling world demand during the recession. However, throughout the post 1973/74 period, the non-oil sector registered very high rates of growth which, in spite of the upswing in world oil demand after 1976, could not be matched by the oil sector. Annual average growth in the non-oil GDP was around 14.5 percent between 1973/74 and 1977/78, compared with 8 percent between 1966/67 and 1972/73.

2.3 STATE OF THE ECONOMY (1978/79 – 1980/81). Most of the trends that began after 1973/74 were still dominant during the years 1978/79 – 1980/81: the non-oil GDP continued to grow at higher rates than the oil sector, business services and construction remained the fastest growing non-oil sectors, and merchandise imports continued to increase by 34-35 percent per year in nominal terms. Two major new developments occurred:

- the policy-induced control of consumer price inflation.
- a considerable increase in both oil production and prices in the fiscal year 1979/80, and a smaller increase in prices accompanied by a slight reduction in oil production in 1980/81.

These developments were caused by factors exogenous to the economy, and were a response to existing conditions in international crude oil markets.

The most dramatic decline in the inflation rate of consumer prices occurred in 1977/78. This rate, which had been 20-30 percent per year during the preceding four fiscal years, dropped to about 5 percent in 1977/78. Even though it increased slightly during 1978/79 and 1979/80, it remained in the single digit range. Much of the reduction in inflation can be attributed to record government spending on food subsidies (which amounted to $451 million for the six months preceding November 1980, against $241 million for the whole of the previous year). Furthermore, the cost of living index excludes most products used by the manufacturing and construction industries, and reflects conditions in the major urban areas only. The GNP deflator, which some regard as a better and less arbitrary indicator of the change in prices, was closer to 9 percent.

Crude oil production, which had remained more or less flat during fiscal 1977/78 and 1978/79, increased sharply (by more than 9 percent to 3.43 billion barrels) in fiscal 1979/80. Given the large contribution of the oil sector to the GDP, this caused a sharp increase in the GDP growth rate, from around 7.7 percent in 1978/79 to 12.2 percent in 1979/80.

Obviously, this sharp rise in the rate of growth of the GDP was in no way indicative of the conditions in the non-oil sector of the domestic economy. The non-oil GDP continued to increase at the high rates of 14.5-15.5 percent per year during the past two fiscal years. However, these and even higher rates had been "normal" for Saudi Arabia since 1973/74.

2.4 RECENT DEVELOPMENTS. The upward pressure on oil prices, which began as a response to the Iranian Revolution and the Iran-Iraq War and was intensified by speculative demand for oil, abated considerably in late 1981. The average price on exports of Saudi crude increased by merely 13.2 percent in 1981 (compared to a 70-percent increase in the previous calendar year). At the same time, crude exports fell slightly in 1981 after two years of continuous increases, during which Saudi Arabia accommodated growing world demand. As a result, the growth in oil revenues slowed down in 1981, bringing pressure on the economy.

Balance of Payments Summary
(SR million)

	1981	1982/1	1983/2
Merchandise trade, fob	274,761	132,480	39,314
Oil exports (excl. bunker oil)	375,320	249,978	150,646
Other exports (excl. re-exports)	541	583	1,727
Imports	-101,100	-118,081	-113,059
Services and transfers	-145,035	-136,247	-93,085
Receipts	**54,916**	**64,966**	**70,736**
Investment income	37,059	48,196	52,631
Oil sector (bunker oil)	1,996	1,124	757
Payments	**-199,951**	**-201,213**	**-163,821**
Freight & insurance	-18,198	-21,254	-20,350
Oil sector investment income	-32,470	-21,291	-11,513
Other private services	-38,747	-38,956	-36,962
Other gov't services	-96,671	-101,855	-77,724
Private transfers	-13,865	-17,857	-17,272
Current Account Balance	**+129,726**	**-3,767**	**-53,771**
Capital Movements & Reserves	**-129,726**	**+3,767**	**+53,771**
Oil sector capital transactions & other capital transactions (net)	+21,811	+38,170	+13,524
Other private capital (net)	+13,013	+16,768	-6,387
Commercial banks (net)	-21,215	-10,738	-5,182
Official capital & reserves	-143,335	-40,433	+51,816

/1 Revised
/2 Preliminary

Source: Saudi Arabian Monetary Agency (SAMA)

In 1982 oil prices began to soften, although prior contractual commitments maintained Saudi prices and in fact permitted a slight (3.6 percent) increase. Output, however, fell sharply (by 35.4 percent) as Saudi Arabia had to absorb much of the shortfall in world demand and buyers for its high-priced crude became scarce. Oil revenues registered substantial declines. The decline continued well into 1983, when exports were nearly halved in the first two quarters, to rally somewhat in the third and fourth quarters. Prices, on the other hand, fell precipitously in 1983, as dissension within OPEC in the face of the international oil glut necessitated cuts in previously set contractual prices.

The steep, steady decline in oil revenue has had a major impact on the rest of the economy. GDP growth, which had fallen to 5.3 percent in 1981, became negative (-4.9 percent) in 1982, and is expected to be an even more alarming -17.1 percent in 1983 (estimates vary widely, however; some claim a recovery has begun in 1983). Meanwhile, the current account balance was upset by shrinking exports and still growing imports; the surplus fell to $4.1 billion in 1982, and became a deficit (estimated at $15.72 million) in 1983. The government budget also began to experience large deficits, as the government felt the need to maintain expenditures at a high level despite falling revenues; the recorded budget surplus for 1981/82 (SR 78.3 billion [$22.9 billion]) dwindled to nearly nothing in 1982/83, and became a deficit (SR 35 billion [$10.15 billion]) in 1983/84. Were it not for the government's willingness to run large deficits, economic growth would be in even more dismal shape.

2.5 SHORT-TERM OUTLOOK. A modest recovery is quite likely as government spending is maintained – spurred, perhaps, by improved conditions in the oil market. GDP growth should resume; it may reach 3 percent in 1984, and stabilize in that neighborhood for some time.

Improved oil market conditions should lead to a reduction in the current account deficit (which should fall to $5 billion in 1984). The deficit should be eliminated and become a surplus by 1985 – assuming import and transfer growth is curbed.

An economic recovery does not signify return to an unlimited growth mentality. Government spending, while maintained in the interest of propping up the economy, is in the process of being "rationalized," with inputs of production beginning to reflect real cost. The age of megaprojects has ended; many gigantic industrial developments are being scaled down or eliminated in the interest of economic efficiency. The mostly likely prognosis is a return to moderate growth rates, with the kingdom moving

Gross Domestic Product by Economic Activity
(at current prices: percents)

Fiscal Year	**1399/1400**	**1400/01**	**1401/02**
Agriculture, Forestry & Fishing	1.2	1.1	1.1
Mining & Quarrying:			
Petroleum & Natural Gas	61.5	56.4	61.6
Other	0.4	0.3	0.4
Manufacturing:			
Petroleum Refining	3.3	4.4	2.5
Other	1.7	1.5	1.7
Electricity, Gas & Water	0.1	0.1	0.1
Construction	11.2	9.7	11.1
Wholesale & Retail Trade Restaurants and Hotels	4.6	4.2	4.8
Transport, Storage, & Communication	4.1	3.3	3.8
Finance, Real Estate, Insurance, & Business Services	4.8	4.3	4.9
Community, Social & Personal Services	1.4	1.1	1.3
Less Imputed Bank Service Charges	-0.9	-0.7	-0.7
Sub-Total	**360,206**	**488,089**	**458,830**
	93.4	93.4	92.6
Government Services:			
Public Administration & Defense	3.5	2.7	3.4
Other Services	2.6	3.0	3.5
Sub-Total	**23,384**	**29,905**	**36,361**
	6.1	5.7	6.9
GDP in Producer's Values	**383,590**	**517,994**	**522,191**
Import Duties	2,217	2,595	2,542
	0.5	0.5	0.5
GDP in Purchaser's Values	**385,807**	**520,589**	**524,733**
	100.0	100.0	100.0

Source: SAMA Statistical Report 1983

slowly toward a modest degree of economic diversification, consolidation of economic ties with other members of the Gulf Cooperation Council, and a larger, better-trained indigenous labor force.

Inflation, which has remained largely under control in the past four years, is unlikely to accelerate; monetary growth has slowed down and is expected to match the level of economic activity as a more energetic central banking authority continues to impose control on the supply of money and credit. The possible phasing out of subsidies (especially on domestically consumed fuel) may result in increases in consumer prices – suggesting that considerable "suppressed" inflationary pressure currently exists.

2.6 SECTORAL BREAKDOWN. The oil and gas sector continues to dominate the economy, and it seems certain that it will continue to do so. It contributed 61.6 percent of GDP in 1981/82, the last year for which reliable statistics exist. The percentage of GDP accounted for over the past five years has varied, largely as a result of fluctuations in the value of oil production by the kingdom, but it has exceeded 50 percent throughout that period.

Construction is the next most important sector. Its role has varied in importance, but it is believed to be currently in decline; demand for construction services has abated as many projects have been completed. It accounted for 11.1 percent of GDP in 1981/82, an increase from the 9.7 percent of the previous fiscal year, but this should not overshadow the downward trend in its contribution to GDP.

As in many Gulf countries, the service (non-commodity producing) sectors have attained a considerable importance, as they are the first to respond to economic growth initiated by government spending. Trade (4.8 percent of GDP in 1981/82) has contributed approximately 5 percent in the past five years; transport (3.8 percent in 1981/82) 3-5 percent, and finance, insurance, real estate and business (4.9 percent combined contribution to GDP in 1981/82) 4-6 percent. No clear trend is discernible in the role of these sectors in GDP, except that (like construction) the total value of their contribution is generally cyclical.

3
DEVELOPMENT PLANNING AND PUBLIC POLICY

3.1 THE FIRST DEVELOPMENT PLAN (1970 – 1974). The First Saudi Development Plan, which appeared in August 1970, was not a detailed economic plan that took all sectors of the economy into consideration. Aside from the fact that the private sector and the oil companies are not considered in it, the Plan only deals with the expenditure allocation of the public sector, and does not employ models or integrated statistical tables to show anticipated availability and use of resources. These drawbacks of the First Plan can be explained to a large degree by the absence of prior planning experience and basic economic statistics in the sixties. In very broad terms, the Plan had three basic objectives: (1) to increase the growth rate of the GDP, (2) to develop human resources, and (3) to diversify the sources of national income and reduce the economy's dependence on oil.

3.2 THE SECOND DEVELOPMENT PLAN (1974/75 – 1979/80). The Second Five-Year Development Plan (1974/75 – 1979/80) was much more detailed and took all the sectors of the economy into consideration. While the development of human resources and diversifying the income base of the economy remained basic objectives, the Plan concentrated on infrastructure formation and was successful in eliminating many of the physical bottlenecks (particularly in the areas of transportation, communications, and residential construction) which had become critical after the 1973/74 oil boom. The other basic achievements were the reduction of acute port congestion, the improvement of labor shortages, and the reduction of the rate of inflation in consumer prices.

One interesting aspect of the performance of the economy during the Second Plan period is that the non-oil sector of the economy surpassed planned targets. Specifically, the planners had underestimated the possible contribution of the private sector to business services.

Even though the overall GDP growth rate between 1974/75 and 1979/80 turned out to be lower than the planned target, sector targets were, in a sense, overachieved. It was the low performance of the oil sector relative to its target that caused the overall GDP growth to be below target. All other sectors of the economy outperformed their planned targets.

3.3 THE THIRD DEVELOPMENT PLAN (1980/81 – 1984/85). The Third Development Plan went into operation in June 1980. The basic guidelines of the Plan indicated a definite change of priorities. The salient points of the Plan include:

- A greater emphasis on resource development, as opposed to infrastructure. The share of allocations to physical infrastructure was reduced from 49.6 percent to 35.5 percent of total development spending, while the share of economic resource development was increased from 25.1 percent to 37.3 percent of total development spending.
- The development of the national labor force through vocational and technical training programs received increasing attention. The share of human resource development rose from 15.9 percent to 18.5 percent of total development spending.
- There was a movement toward decentralization in order to ensure a more even geographic distribution of wealth. Allocations to municipalities, for instance, were increased, and several regional industrial centers (away from the main urban agglommerations) are envisaged.
- To promote the goal of self-sufficiency in food, the Plan called for considerable agricultural development, as well as development of the Kingdom's fisheries.
- Improvement in social services, especially health care and housing, was projected. "A better quality of life" for Saudi citizens was identified as one of the major goals of the Plan.

3.4 ASSESSMENT OF PERFORMANCE. Saudi Arabia's past record of plan implementation shows a tendency toward overfulfillment of targets on the expenditure side. The First Plan had a budget of $17 billion; actual expenditures turned out to be $23.4 billion. Under the Second Plan, total planned expenditures were estimated at $150 billion, and the actual expenditure is estimated to have exceeded $210 billion. The budgeted and expected actual expenditures of the Third Plan are $250 billion and more than $300 billion respectively.

It is difficult to assess the performance of the First Plan, not only because it did not have well-defined targets, but also because the oil shock of 1973/74 completely changed the pattern of oil revenues and expenditures. This development could not have been anticipated in 1970 when the Plan was issued.

The performance of the Second Plan can be considered a success. Its achievements include:

- Improvement in the labor situation. The shortage of labor was especially acute in 1975 and again in 1977. The planned importation of Asian workers (mainly Koreans and Filipinos) has more or less remedied the problem, at least for the moment. The high percentage of foreign workers (70 percent of the 2.5 million workforce) is still a serious problem.
- Reduction of port congestion. The ports were unusually congested in mid-1976 and again in mid-1977. This problem has been largely eliminated.
- The inflation rate, which reached 40 percent in the mid-1970s, has been reduced to single-digit levels through monetary controls and food subsidies.
- Expatriate workers are now better housed. This was one of the objectives of the Plan in order to avoid possible political tension. Generally speaking, foreign workers are better housed in Saudi Arabia than they are in other Gulf countries.

Evaluating the performance of the nearly completed Third Plan is problematic. First, a number of projects executed in the context of the Plan have a long gestation period – particularly those which focus on manpower development; it is simply too early to judge the success of such programs. Second, the spectacular fluctuations in government revenue created serious complications for Saudi Arabia. Given the demonstrated instability of the Kingdom's long-range earning power, the scale of the Third Plan had to be revised repeatedly. At the same time, it was necessary to avoid dramatic changes in the level of government spending to avoid destabilizing the domestic economy. As a result, long- (or even medium-) range planning became exceedingly difficult; more, fluctuations in government expenditures or the promptitude of government payments were dictated so often by relatively short-term political and financial considerations that long-term economic considerations appeared subordinated to transient phenomena.

The challenge facing Saudi planners is still a formidable one. In particular:

- It is recognized that the goal of economic diversification is a long way from being achieved. Neither the agricultural nor the non-oil manufacturing sector is significant yet; while the development of oil- and gas-related industries has proceeded more or less according to plan, conditions in world-wide energy markets are such that, rather than contribute to economic diversification, such development could create serious problems for the Kingdom.
- Rapid growth in the past decade has increased dependence on foreign manpower. The percentage of non-Arabs (notably Asians) has been allowed to increase, to the point of creating social and cultural problems.
- The goal of self-sufficiency in food is elusive. Wheat production has increased dramatically, but at cost far in excess of the cost of importation. Meanwhile, the water table is dropping (by as much as 60 m in some cases), raising the specter of suggesting rapid depletion through inefficient irrigation. Also, there are not enough silos for the grain already being produced.
- The role of the private sector has yet to become significant. While a fair amount of private sector participation in the areas of agriculture, light industry and services has been recorded, government spending is still the driving force in the economy. The level and pattern of economic activity is largely dictated by the size and composition of the government budget.

The Saudi experience in planning has demonstrated that an abundance of funds and foreign exchange is not enough to insure balanced economic development. Such considerations as the absorptive capacity of the economy, the role of private sector initiative, the scarcity of resources and the feasibility (and desirability) of developing such resources remain paramount.

3.5 THE FOURTH PLAN (1985/86 – 1990/91). The allocations for the Fourth Five-Year Plan (1985-90) have not yet been released. However, the Ministry of Planning has indicated that the following objectives will be stressed in determining priorities and allocations:

- Expanding and improving the quality of the domestic labor force.
- Reducing dependence on crude oil production and export as the primary contributor to GDP.
- Continuing the process of economic diversification, particularly through the development of the manufacturing and agricultural sectors.
- Encouraging eploration for and development of the Kingdom's mineral resources.
- Completing the development of the Kingdom's physical infrastructure.
- Promoting economic and social complementarity among the member states of the Gulf Cooperation Council.

The last objective is a new one which could assume considerable significance if treated as a priority. It would presumably imply greater coordination in planning, avoidance of duplication in development projects, and freer movement of capital and labor.

The Ministry of Planning has indicated that the following considerations will be of major importance:

- Private sector participation will be encouraged.
- Rationalization (the policy of authorizing only those allocations which can be justified in cost-benefit terms) is the order of the day, particularly in regard to subsidies.
- Stricter economic criteria will be employed in assessing government projects, emphasis being placed on the real cost of inputs and efficient use of economic resources.
- Oil- and gas-related industries will receive considerable attention, vertical integration and expansion of refining capacity being a priority.
- Monetary policy will seek to match expenditure with state revenue, due consideration being given to the costs of project maintenance (expected to account for some 30 percent of allocated spending) and operation, in addition to construction costs.

3.6 THE BUDGET. Of far greater significance than the outline of the Five Year Plan in determining the thrust of government policy and priorities is the annual budget, which reflects the impact of current developments on the formulation of fiscal policy, and is itself a major determinant of the level and pattern of aggregate spending throughout the economy.

The actual level of government spending in fiscal 1983/84 fell short of the projected SR 260 billion ($74.29 billion), amounting to SR 222 billion ($63.43 billion). This was a reflection of revenues proving to be lower than anticipated: SR 187 billion ($53.43 billion), compared with a projected SR 225 billion ($64.29 billion). The actual budget deficit, however, corresponded to projections, amounting to SR 35 billion ($10.00 billion). This pattern is revealing.

- It indicates that actual government spending is highly responsive to unanticipated fluctuations in government revenue.
- It indicates that the government assigns a high priority to the impact (stimulatory in this case) of its fiscal operations on aggregate demand. Spending was maintained at a level that ensured the size of the deficit in 1983/84 would correspond to the projected amount, thus ensuring the desired degree of fiscal stimulation. In determining the amount to be spent on projects, the government is at least as concerned with the impact such spending has on economic activity as with the benefits from the project itself.

The recently released 1984/85 budget projects a deficit of SR 45.9 billion ($13.11 billion). It is apparent that the government is concerned with the slowdown of economic activity, and intends to boost it through deficit financing, even at the cost of drawing down reserves.

The level of revenue forecast in the 1984/85 budget (SR 214.1 billion [$61.17 billion], lower than the SR 225 billion [$64.29 billion] initially projected for 1983/84 but higher than the actual SR 187 billion [$53.43 billion] which did accrue) is conservative in view of the modest recovery in the international oil market. (However, disruption of oil shipments due to heightened tensions in the Gulf could make this estimate optimistic.) The level of expenditure is projected at SR 260 billion ($74.29 billion), the same level that had been projected for 1983/84.

Capital spending is projected at SR 111.7 billion ($31.78 billion), or 43 percent of total expenditure – a reassuring signal to the depressed construction sector. Administrative costs, however, will be kept at roughly the same level as the in 1983/84. The areas of greatest increase in allocation are in health (62 percent increase for Health Ministry spending on projects and maintenance) and education (74 percent increase in the allocation to King Saud University, now projected at SR 3.3 billion [$938.8 million]). Provincial development schemes continue to receive priority treatment; developments are planned in Jizan, Qunfudah and Lith on the Red Sea. Among the major losers are the Saline Water Conversion Corporation (a reduction of more than 30 percent in its allocation to SR 2.7 billion [$768.1 million]) and transport and communications (whose allocation is 5 percent lower than in 1983/84).

The allocation to human resources will drop very slightly (0.5 percent), a reflection of previous difficulties in spending the full amount allocated (there was underspending of 11.2 percent of the 1983/84 allocation) rather than de-emphasis by planners. Defense spending is still the largest item, accounting for 29.6 percent of the budget (its allocation is boosted by 5.5 percent, a reflection of continued concern about regional instability). Social development will get a considerable boost (a 33 percent increase), reflecting continued commitment to a better quality of life. Infrastructural allocations will grow modestly (2.6 percent). Economic resource development will register a considerable increase, much of the increase going to the Industry and Electricity Ministry.

Few details on the revenue side are available, other than a projected total of SR 214.1 million ($60.91 million). In the 1983/84 budget, the last one for which a breakdown of revenue sources was available, SR 153.4 million ($43.64 million) was projected in oil income (68.2 percent of the projected total), with SR 45.4 million ($12.91 million) projected in investment income (20.2 percent of the projected total). Other sources of revenue include customs duties and fees collected for the use of postal, telegraphic and telecommunications services.

The deficit will be financed by drawing on the Kingdom's General Reserves, which are considerable. Nonetheless, Saudi planners are becoming much more sensitive to fiscal pressures, as evidenced by their determination to keep administrative costs under control, as well as clear indications that some subsidies are being phased out: the Ministry of Finance has called for an increase of up to 70 percent in the price of domestically – produced gasoline (from SR 0.29 to SR 0.49 a liter), to begin on the first day of the fiscal year. The purpose of such a step is to curb the wasteful consumption of the Kingdom's resources and to rationalize government spending.

4
PETROLEUM SECTOR

4.1 SAUDI OIL RESERVES. Saudi Arabia enjoys the largest proven petroleum reserves to be found in any single country in the world and these account for around one-quarter of total world reserves. Moreover, in every year since 1960, additions to the estimates of Saudi Arabia's proven reserves exceeded its annual production totals. While estimates of proven reserves vary, the figure of 165 billion barrels is quoted by ARAMCO, the major producing company for the area under its control. (Figures for the small areas assigned to Getty and Arabian Oil are approximately 3 billion barrels of reserves). It is thought that Saudi Arabia has a maximum sustainable capacity in crude oil production of between 10 and 11 mbd, including its share of production in the Neutral Zone. Probable reserves in the ARAMCO-retained areas alone were estimated at 177.2 billion barrels in 1981.

At 1983 average production rates (approximately 5 mbd, which corresponds to the most recent OPEC quota assigned to Saudi Arabia in March 1983), Saudi Arabia's proven reserves should last 89 years.

4.2 GAS RESERVES AND INDUSTRY. Saudi gas reserves are estimated by ARAMCO at 3.2 trillion cu m (114 trillion cu ft). Gas production fell by more than 50 percent in 1982 to 9.02 billion cu m (318.54 billion cu ft) from 19.58 billion cu m (691.46 billion cu ft) in 1981 – reflection of the shortfall in associated natural gas that followed from the cutback in oil production. Saudi Arabia's exports of LPG to Japan (the main buyer of Saudi LPG) fell to 2.704 million tons (from 3.377 million tons in 1981) as a result of restricted gas availability. At the same time, LPG prices were cut several times (in line with the cut in the cost of oil) to satisfy Japanese customers. Saudi Arabia remains the largest Gulf exporter of LPG to Japan, the UAE being a distant second.

The cutbacks in oil production have led to such a severe shortage of associated gas that not only is LPG production suffering, but also the supply of electricity within the Kingdom – to the point that a 24-hour blackout hit the Eastern Provine in June 1983. Norbec, a subsidiary of Petromin, was set up in Zug, Switzerland to market 200,000 b/d of oil on the spot market specifically to ensure that enough Saudi crude was being marketed to produce the necessary associated gas. In addition, steps were taken by ARAMCO to develop non-associated gas from the Permian Khuff formation (with a potential 28.32 million cu m/day capacity [1 billion cu ft/day]); most of the wells were expected to go on stream in August 1984.

4.3 DEVELOPMENT AND ORGANIZATION OF THE OIL AND GAS INDUSTRY. The first exploration concession to a foreign firm was granted in 1923 to a British syndicate, but nothing came of it. In 1933, a new company was formed (California Arabian Standard Oil Company, or CASOC) to exploit a concession granted to Socal. Texaco aquired a stake in CASOC before production began in 1938 at the Dammam field in the Eastern Province. A refinery at Ras Tanura started operations in 1941.

In 1944, CASOC was renamed Arabian American Oil Company (ARAMCO). In 1948, Standard Oil of New Jersey (later Exxon) and Socon-Vacuum Oil Company (Mobil) acquired a share in ARAMCO. Production expanded rapidly. By 1950 Tapline, an oil pipeline, was completed. Associated natural gas was liquefied, with exports of LPG beginning in 1961. The first offshore gas/oil separation plant (GOSP) was opened at Sanafiya in 1969.

The seventies saw a major reorganization of the oil industry in Saudi Arabia. At the beginning of 1973, Petromin (General Petroleum and Mineral Organization, the state oil company) acquired a 25-percent stake in ARAMCO concessions and operations. The 1973 oil embargo and the escalation in oil prices convinced the government of the necessity to control production; Petromin's stake in ARAMCO was raised to 60 percent at the beginning of 1974.

The government asked ARAMCO to develop gas gathering facilities throughout the Kingdom. In 1977, ARAMCO was awarded a five-year contract to operate SCECO-East (Saudi Consolidated Electric Company for the Eastern Province). The Saudiization of ARAMCO concessions and operations was completed in 1980 with retroactive effect as Petromin acquired the remaining shares in ARAMCO. The ARAMCO-SCECO contract was extended in 1982.

ARAMCO (28.3 percent of which is currently owned by Exxon, Standard Oil of California, and Texaco, and 15 percent by Mobil) still plays a role in Saudi oil production. It provides Petromin with technical assistance on a per-barrel fee basis, and has access (at pre-negotiated prices) to crude ouput in excess of Petromin's sales and refining needs. This arrangement was profitable to ARAMCO owners while spot prices were escalating in 1979 and 1980, but it proved unprofitable in 1982 and 1983, when spot prices fell well below contractual prices. It was announced recently that ARAMCO will be getting its first Saudi president this year; Ali Naimi (first vice-president of operations) is slated to succeed the retiring incumbent.

Petromin, the state oil company, now has monopoly of local oil product distribution, participates on a sole or majority ownership basis in all refineries whose output is earmarked for the local market, and is to have equal share in export-oriented refineries. Petromin's subsidiary, Petroship, does not have monopoly over overseas shipping (as in many other Gulf states). The total capacity of Petroship's fleet was raised to 180,000 dwt recently with the acquisition of two Japanese product tankers. Petromin also has a 51 percent interest in the Saudi Arabian Fertilizer Company (the remaining 49 percent is in Saudi private hands), but it has been decided that all other petrochemical projects will be administered by SABIC (the Saudi Arabian Basic Industries Corporation).

4.4 PRODUCTION AND PRICING POLICIES: STRENGTHS AND CONSTRAINTS. Saudi Arabia is in a position to exercise considerable influence in international oil markets, the reasons for this being:

- Saudi Arabia has a high (10-11 mbd) oil production capacity, giving it the power to increase the supply of oil dramatically, as it did in 1979 and 1980.
- Saudi Arabia's huge financial reserves give it the power to meet financial needs while maintaining relatively low oil production levels.

This has put Saudi Arabia in the position of acting as "swing (marginal) producer," fine tuning its own production level to bring about desired conditions in international oil markets. At the same time, Saudi Arabia's flexibility in setting production and pricing policies for its crude is limited by the following considerations:

- The Kingdom's ambitious developing needs require considerable, long-range financial commitments;

revenue shortfalls exert fiscal pressures if sustained for a lengthy period.

- Saudi Arabia's burgeoning petrochemical (and notably gas liquefaction) industries are adversely affected by severely depressed output, which reduces domestically produced (cheap) feedstock.
- A serious disruption in oil shipments through the Gulf would seriously limit the role Saudi Arabia can play in international oil markets, as other outlets for their crude (e.g. the pipeline to Yanbu) have a limited capacity.
- Much of Saudi Arabia's financial wealth is invested in OECD countries; as Saudi trade with the eastern bloc is practically non-existent, Saudi Arabia needs a prosperous west if it is to sell enough of its crude to implement its development policies. It is not in Saudi Arabia's interest to see ruinous increases in oil prices cause economic chaos in the west.
- The long expected lifespan of Saudi oil reserves means it is not in the Kingdom's interest for oil prices to remain prohibitively high for a long time. This would encourage the development of alternate sources of energy, reducing the value of future Saudi oil production. The recent fall in oil prices may be construed as in the Kingdom's long-term interest.

The objectives of Saudi Arabia's oil production and pricing policies may therefore be summarized as follows:

- Maintaining orderly conditions in international oil markets.
- Maintaining (on a long-term basis) a high enough level of production to meet long-term financial and feedstock needs.
- Maximizing long-term revenues from oil <u>and</u> financial investments.

The degree of Saudi sophistication in pursuing a long-term foreign investment strategy seems lower than that of the Kuwaitis, suggesting that the Saudis assign a secondary importance to international investment policies.

Saudi Arabia's habitual moderation in oil policy has not only created tension between the Kingdom and other OPEC members; it has raised questions from factions within the Saudi ruling circle concerning the optimal extent of such moderation. There are indications that some factions are opposed to current Saudi over-production, and would favor a more balanced oil policy – one which, while taking into consideration the economic and political welfare of the west, will not disregard the domestic economic and political stability of the Kingdom.

4.5 PRODUCTION AND PRICING: THE RECORD. Saudi Arabia's generally moderate attitude in oil production and pricing has often led to conflict, and sometimes direct confrontation, with other OPEC members. One such occasion occurred in 1977. At the December 1976 OPEC meeting, Saudi Arabia and the United Arab Emirates proposed to raise prices by 5 percent in January 1977, and to keep prices frozen for the rest of the year. This scheme found strong opposition from all the other OPEC members who pushed for a 10 percent increase in January, followed by a 5 percent increase in July. When the latter went ahead with their 10 percent initial increase, Saudi Arabia threatened to, and then actually did, boost production in order to "flood the market" and prevent the other members of OPEC from carrying out their pricing schedule. Oil production jumped from 8.57 mbd in 1976 to 9.32 mbd in the first quarter of 1977 and to 9.4 mbd in the second quarter of 1977. While this did create a surplus in international oil markets, it was not large enough to allow Saudi Arabia to have its way. In June the two opposing groups decided to meet halfway: Saudi Arabia increased its price by another 5 percent, and the remaining members of OPEC upped their planned 5 percent increase in July.

The Saudi government's response to the 1979 and 1980 oil crises is another case in point. Before the outbreak of the Iranian Revolution and the subsequent crude oil shortages, the government had imposed a production ceiling on the Arabian-American Oil Company (ARAMCO) of 8.5 mbd. This restriction was removed and production by ARAMCO was raised to alleviate part of the shortage. Saudi production peaked at an average 9.9 mbd in 1981 (production exceeded 10.5 mbd in certain months of that year), as Saudi Arabia responded to the shortfall in supply brought about by the Iranian revolution and the outbreak of the Iran-Iraq War. Demand accelerated concurrently, much of it for stockpiling purposes.

Average daily production dropped slightly (to 9.8 mbd) in 1981, although there were clear signs that supply was shortly to increase and demand to decline as stockpiling capacity was exhausted. There are many interpretation's of Saudi Arabia's willingness to continue producing at a high rate over that period; the one advanced by Saudi officials is that they acted out of a sense of obligation to the west.

Saudi pricing policy continued to be moderate. In spite of the fact that oil prices had tripled on the spot market, and oil producers had repeatedly imposed premiums over the official contract prices, the Saudi price remained $4-$5 per barrel below the OPEC average for a long time. Until the last quarter of 1981, Saudi crude never sold at more than $32 a barrel (against $34 charged by most oil exporters). The price of Saudi crude was finally raised to $34, on the understanding that OPEC prices would remain frozen through the end of 1982.

The Saudis' fear of higher prices proved groundless. Indeed, as demand fell and Iran nearly doubled its average production level in 1982, the pressure on prices was reversed. With widespread "cheating" from OPEC members, notably Iran and Nigeria (who resorted to production in excess of quotas and considerable official and semi-official discounting to increase falling revenues), Saudi Arabia found itself under pressure to cut production to prevent a price collapse. It duly obliged the rest of OPEC, largely in the interest of market stability, although the damage to Saudi interests from lower revenues and lower production levels was not inconsiderable. Average production dropped to 6.5 mbd in 1982 and to 5 mbd in 1983. Saudi restraint did not save the price level OPEC had hoped to be able to maintain; it proved necessary to cut international prices to $32 (from $34) in the spring of 1983, and Saudi Arabia had to resign itself to a production level of 5 mbd (which became its official quota in March 1983) for the foreseeable future. That meant Saudi Arabia was to continue practicing restraint, while OPEC cheaters (particularly Iran) reaped the benefits.

4.6 CONSUMPTION OF ENERGY. Saudi Arabia's domestic consumption of energy has been growing rapidly in the past few years. Over the period 1970 – 80, energy consumption is estimated to have grown at an average 30 percent annually, a higher rate than in nearly all other OPEC producers. This rapid increase in energy consumption has been attributed to:

- A high population growth rate, supplemented by accelerated immigration.
- Rapidly increasing income levels among the population, which, coupled with exposure to foreign influences, increased demand for electric appliances, some of which came to be regarded as virtual

necessities. The result has been a higher rate of electricity usage.

- Rapid industrialization, which generated higher energy needs both for the production process and for such necessities as transportation and storage.
- Heavy subsidization of fuel for consumption and industrial purposes, resulting in considerable inefficiency in its use.

Consumption of petroleum products in 1982 was estimated at 451,200 b/d, up 8.3 percent from 1981. In tons of oil equivalent, the 1980 energy usage rate of 28,138 toe can be broken down into: 18,159 toe in oil and oil products, and 9,979 toe in gas. By the year 2000, energy usage is expected by experts to rise to 112,000 mbd (78,000 mbd of oil and oil products and 34,000 mbd of gas). This suggests an average annual growth rate of 10.4 percent for 1980 – 90 and 4.0 percent thereafter, the reduction in growth rates being brought about by greater efficiency (fostered by lowered subsidies) and by the saturation point having been reached in the case of many consumer products.

The rapid increase in consumption can, nonetheless, result in serious problems for Saudi Arabia. Not only does inefficient use of energy represent a waste of the Kingdom's resources, but Saudi Arabia's ability to manipulate developments in the international oil market can be affected if consumer demand grows while productive capacity remains the same. In addition to reducing subsidies to encourage conservation, the government is intent upon developing solar energy (in which it has obvious advantages).

4.7 OIL- AND GAS-RELATED INDUSTRIES. Saudi Arabia has made major strides in developing its petrochemical industries. Oil refining capacity is expanding rapidly; Saudi Arabia is expected to be exporting 520,000 b/d by 1990. Expansion of refinery capacity has been a major priority, and an integral part of industrial development schemes; both Yanbu and Jubayl are to have refineries (all managed by Petromin) for domestically consumed oil products and for export. Saudi Arabia is likely to encounter considerable difficulties in marketing its refined crude, unless it follows Kuwait's example in acquiring retail outlets abroad – which could herald an era of competition between producers of refined products. At present, it appears that, unlike Kuwait, Saudi Arabia has opted for cooperating with the international oil companies, who are to take an equity share in the domestic refining companies and in return provide expertise, training and most of the necessary marketing outlets – a cautious, non-confrontational approach.

Petroline, a major (1,200 km) pipeline connecting the oilfields in the Eastern Province to the port of Yanbu on the Red Sea has been operational for nearly two years. Petroline's capacity is to be boosted from 1.85 mbd to 2.8 mbd as pumping stations are installed along its route; an additional pipeline will connect it to the Iraqi oil fields near Basra (at a cost of some $3 billion). The advantage of this network is reduced reliance (for Saudi Arabia and Iraq) on the increasingly precarious Gulf for transportation of oil. It proved necessary to halve the transit fee through Petroline last year; only 0.3 mbd of its 1.85 mbd capacity was being utilized because the transit fee ($0.50 per barrel) made it too expensive to ship oil through Petroline. Tapline, which once connected the Saudi oilfields to Lebanon, has long been closed.

5
AGRICULTURAL SECTOR

5.1 CURRENT CONDITIONS. The contribution of the agriculture, forestry and fishing sector has been declining in recent years. In fiscal 1981/82, it accounted for 1.1 percent of GDP at current prices (3.4 percent of GDP at constant 1979/80 prices). Its share was approximately the same in the previous year, but had been higher in 1977/78 and 1978/79 (approximately 1.7 percent at current prices).

This development is largely a reflection of the rapid rise in GDP (dominated by oil income) through 1982. It should not overshadow the fact that the agricultural sector has been growing quite rapidly in the past few years (at an average 8 percent in the five years up to 1980/81). In the case of certain crops, production has risen dramatically. Wheat production, in particular, increased from a mere 3,300 tons in 1977 to 600,000 tons in 1982 and 1983; domestic wheat production now meets nearly 86 percent of estimated domestic demand, with production in 1984/85 expected to cover the projected demand of 800,000 tons. Similar progress has been made in poultry production and water-resource development. Experts predict that Saudi Arabia will have attained near-self-sufficiency in wheat production by 1985. By the year 2000, most experts expect Saudi Arabia to be nearly 90 percent self-sufficient in white meat, 50 percent self-sufficient in fish, and 30 percent self-sufficient in dairy products.

Given continued government support, it seems likely that the agricultural sector will not be adversely affected by fiscal pressures and the overall economic slowdown – despite the formidable constraints on its development.

The agricultural sector employed 24.2 percent of the economically active population in 1979/80, making it the largest single employer. This represents a significant drop from the 1974/75 level (39.8 percent), reflecting the movement of many workers formerly employed in agriculture to the more profitable construction and service sectors.

5.2 CONSTRAINTS ON DEVELOPMENT. The development of agriculture is limited by a number of resource and other constraints. These include:

- Water scarcity. Sources of water are extremely limited. In particular:

  - o There are no permanent rivers or fresh water bodies anywhere in Saudi Arabia.
  - o Only 3 percent of the Kingdom (all of it in the Asir region along a narrow hilly belt extending from Taif to the border with the Yemen Arab Republic) receives more than 200 mm of rainfall annually, some 40-50 percent of which is in summer. As the altitude mitigates the temperature, a certain amount of rainfed agriculture is possible, although supplementary irrigation is often necessary. In such areas, land and water rights are inseparable. Elsewhere, rainfall is usually lower than 100 mm annually, much of it in the summer, when the intense heat results in very high evaporation rates. Only 20 percent of the very limited cultivated area is rainfed.
  - o The rest of the cultivated area is dependent on irrigation from wells, pits, subterranean canals or springs. As water obtained from such sources is extremely limited, water rights are separate from (and usually more important than) land ownership rights; they can be bought, rented or inherited separately. In areas that are not rainfed, irrigation entails flooding the land with water drawn from underground sources by animal power or diesel pumps. Large artesian wells are used in the eastern province (usually to irrigate date- and rice-producing areas). Horizontal underground water canals (known as kharaz or dabbles) are used in areas on the Red Sea plain and (to a lesser extent) in the eastern province; they are reportedly becoming obsolete.
  - o Underground water is only partially renewable; if water is drawn at a more rapid rate than the aquifer is recharged, the water table falls. The water table in the eastern province has dropped 12 m. Fossil water (which comprises 75 percent of Saudi Arabia's water reserves, and meets most of the water needs of the western province) is entirely non-renewable, and is being depleted rapidly. Concern about the rapid depletion of water resources has prompted the government to ban unauthorized

well-drilling, causing many firms to cut back drilling activities and so reducing the supply of water for current use. It is often necessary to dig very deep for water: from 500 m downward. This entails considerable cost.

- Soil infertility is a serious limitation, although not as binding as water scarcity. The best soils for cultivation in Saudi Arabia are alluvial soils. This, coupled with the availability of shallow groundwater, spurred the growth of the two great oases of al-Hasa and Qatif. A number of wadis, extending fanwise along the sedimentary basin, also comprise zones of deep, high-quality alluvial soils; where groundwater was accessible through wells or artesian springs, scattered oases have developed – notably in Najd (in the proximity of Riyadh) and in Qassim. Nearly 40 percent of the country and more than half of the sedimentary area is covered by mobile sand dunes. Much of country is largely uncultivable; what little vegetation it supports is seasonal and often unpredictable. This is particularly true of the Rub al-Khali (Empty Quarter, extending from the border with the Yemen Arab Republic to the Arabian Gulf), in whose northern and eastern fringes some seasonal grasses grow, the Nafud Desert in the north (which contains a few scattered oases and supports some winter and spring grazing vegetation), and the Dahna Desert separating Najd from the Eastern Province (which supports even less winter and spring grazing vegetation).
- Adverse climatic conditions exist. Summer temperatures in the desert regions often rise above 49° C (120° F), making the growing of many crops impossible during that season, and contributing to the extremely high water evaporation rate. Diurnal variations in some areas (notably the Nafud Desert) can be as high as 45 degrees during the summer. Frost can exist in winter in the Northern Desert.
- The pattern of land tenure complicates long-range planning and nearly precludes economies of scale. The average agricultural unit is between 2.02 and 5.06 ha in Asir and the eastern province, the most productive areas agriculturally, and between 5.06 and 20.23 ha in Najd. Single units of more than 101.2 ha are unusual. Much of the land is leased to farmers on a share-cropping basis, with the period of the lease often no more than one year.
- Labor is expensive and sometimes scarce, largely as a

result of the small population base and the temptation to work in the industrial and service sectors, which pay better. As a result, it has often been necessary to employ foreigners, whose cost is considerable if they possess farming skills.

- Competition from foreign producers of vegetables (notably Holland, France and Belgium) is quite intense, creating a serious problem for the burgeoning domestic greenhouse business.
- Data on market requirements is scarce, and there is little coordination between producers. This often creates problems of oversupply, which are made worse by the lack of adequate storage facilities (particularly cold storage facilities for dairy products).

It should be noted that the scarcity of water is by far the worst of these problems. Estimates conducted in the late sixties suggested that the cultivable area in the Kingdom totalled 4.2 million ha (compared to the then cultivated area of 385,000 ha if only soil and terrain criteria were employed. If water availability were taken into consideration, the same survey showed that the potential for expansion would be much reduced: to 82,550 ha, an expansion of only about 20 percent.

5.3 GOVERNMENT SUPPORT. The Saudi government is strongly committed to the development of the agricultural sector. Its motives can be summarized as follows:

- The government wishes to improve the standard of living in the traditionally agricultural areas, which continue to employ a large percentage of the economically active population.
- Food imports to meet domestic demand represent a major drain: in 1982/83 they were estimated at SR 9.5 billion ($2.75 billion) (out of total private sector imports of SR 71.2 billion [$20.64 billion]). While Saudi Arabia is hardly subject to a foreign exchange constraint, the fact remains that such massive expenditure on food imports represents a waste of resources in the case of those crops which can be produced economically at home. It also heightens the Kingdom's dependence on foreign suppliers, increasing Saudi Arabia's vulnerability to a food boycott and to year-to-year fluctuations in crop conditions in foreign countries.

Government support for the agricultural sector is usually channelled through the Saudi Arabian Agricultural Bank (SAAB) in Riyadh. Under the Third Plan, $1.5 billion are earmarked for agricultural loans and $0.75 billion for subsidies. Funds are channelled through SAAB primarily through:

- Interest-free loans of 80 percent of the cost of an agricultural project up to $1.5 million (and 60 percent up to $6 million). Loans for inputs are for one year and for equipment for a period varying between five and ten years, with a two-year grace period.
- Subsidies of 50 percent of the cost of fertilizers and 100 percent of the cost of pesticides.
- Subsidies of 20-30 percent of the cost of equipment for poultry and dairy farms, and 40-50 percent on selected farming equipment.
- Subsidies on purchases of date palms and seed potato.
- Subsidies of 100 percent on the air freight cost of importing cattle, provided at least fifty head are imported at one time.

Lending by SAAB increased sharply in 1980/81, when increased oil revenue increased the availability of funds and sharply accelerated the growth rate of consumption demand. By 1981/82, lending by SAAB totalled SR 2.932 billion ($833.2 million), a 161 percent increase from the amount of two years earlier. The region of Buraidah (in the central Qassim Province) accounted for the largest share of SAAB lending (SR 560 million [$163.98 million]), followed by al-Kharj, near Riyadh (SR 553 million [$161.93 million]), Riyadh (SR 448 million [$131.19 million]) and Taif (SR 288 million [$84.33 million]). Poultry projects received the biggest share of bank lending (25.4 percent), followed by well-drilling and casing (14 percent) and tractors and agricultural machinery (13.8 percent).

In addition, the government issued a Public Land Distribution Ordinance (PLDO) in 1968, promoting the horizontal expansion of agriculture in the Kingdom by making landholding units of varying sizes (up to 500 ha) available to suitable applicants, and up to 1,619 ha in exceptional cases. By 1980, about 123,000 ha of public land had been distributed to 19,400 individuals and 87 large projects.

The government is also taking steps (through the Ministry of Agriculture and Water) to meet future water needs. This is becoming particularly critical, as the following developments are anticipated:

- Urban industrial use of water, which stood at 502 million cu m annually, is expected to grow rapidly (to a projected 2.279 billion cu m annually in 1999/2000) as a result of the expanding industrial sector, population growth, and the increasing reliance on brackish water in the process of reinjection of water into the oilfields to maintain oil extraction rates.
- Irrigated agricultural use of water is also expected to grow from 1.832 billion cu m annually in 1979/80 to 3.220 billion cu m annually in 1999/2000, as the sector continues its growth.

To meet the growing demand, the government is relying on desalination. By 1999/2000, 1.198 billion cu m will be produced through desalination. Additional water (730 million cu m annually) is to be made available through effluent reclamation.

5.4 CROP DISTRIBUTION. Dates are produced in Medina and the Najd, and in various localities throughout the Kingdom, notably near Najran in the south, throughout the Eastern Province, and at oases at Hail, al-Jauf, Taima and Ala. The products of the Najd also include staples such as wheat and barley in addition to livestock. Taif and other oases produce honey and fruit. The bedouin specialize in livestock raising.

In 1979/80 (the last year for which accurate statistics are available), 441,000 tons of dates, 218,00 tons of tomatoes, 215,000 tons of sorghum, and 158,000 tons of wheat were produced. During that same year, 405,000 ha were allocated to the cultivation of sorghum, 84,000 to wheat production, 68,000 to date production and 21,000 to tomato production. Onions had the highest yield in tons per ha (25.6), followed by tomatoes (10.3) and watermelons (10.2).

Other important crops include barley, millet, eggplant, grapes, and citrus fruits.

5.5 LIVESTOCK AND FISHERIES. Livestock rearing is the traditional bedouin occupation, the limited vegetation in the scattered oases and other arable spots being ideal for grazing. Livestock and poultry rearing are assuming increasing importance, primarily because;

- They draw on already existing skills and resources.
- They contribute to the goal of self-sufficiency in food.
- Livestock rearing enterprises can be started easily through heavily subsidized importation of cattle and poultry.
- Livestock and poultry rearing enterprises can be run as large-scale commercial operations. (Few private-sector enterprises can boast this advantage in Saudi Arabia.)

SAADCO (Saudi Arabian Agricultural and Dairy Company), established in 1977, has invested heavily in a dairy farm at Kharj (near Riyadh) which was projected by its owners to become the largest in the Middle East. The SAADCO herd of 25,000 cows was to have provided Riyadh with fresh dairy products, to be spurred by the construction of the Eastern Province highway. SAADCO was able to raise a substantial sum (SR 240 million [$69.8 million]) in a loan syndicated by the Saudi Investment Banking Corporation (SIBC) By early 1983, however, SAADCO found itself in a financial bind, brought about by disagreements between managers over pricing and production policies. This resulted in SAADCO defaulting on an interst payment of SR 19 million ($5.52 million).

SAADCO's difficulties, being managerial in nature, are not symptomatic of the condition of livestock and dairy production in Saudi Arabia. Saudi Arabia has, in fact, made impressive progress in the poultry and livestock sector. In 1980, the 157 broiler units and 146 egg-laying units (financed by SAAB loans totalling SR 473 million [$142.26 million]) met 19 percent of domestic demand for poultry and 76 percent of demand for eggs. Additional SAAB loans were granted in subsequent years (the largest share of SAAB loans went to poultry projects, which were deemed potentially the most profitable). Dairy production is likewise expanding, with a number of turnkey dairies being imported from Denmark.

6
INDUSTRIAL SECTOR

6.1 GENERAL CONDITIONS. There are, at present, no significant non-oil manufacturing industries in Saudi Arabia. The share of non-oil industries other than petroleum refining has fluctuated slightly in recent years, peaking at 2.1 percent in 1978/79, and then declining, to stand at 1.7 percent in 1981/82, the last year for which reliable GDP statistics are available. Mining and quarrying of minerals has traditionally accounted for about one half of 1 percent of GDP; its share of GDP was 0.4 percent in 1981/82. Revenue generated by the industrial sector (defined to include petrochemical industries) was estimated officially at SR 20 billion ($5.7 billion) in fiscal 1983/84.

The non-oil industrial sector is not a major employer. The number of workers in the manufacturing industries and in mining has increased considerably in recent years (a reflection of relatively high wages, which lured many workers from the agricultural sector). Total employment in manufacturing was estimated at 104,200 in 1979/80, giving the manufacturing sector a share of 4.2 percent of total employment, which is the same share it had five years earlier. Mining employed 7,300 workers in 1979/80 – 0.3 percent of the labor force, which represent a minimal increase from the 0.2 percent share it had five years earlier.

6.2 EXPANSION ENCOURAGED. In recent years, the government has tried vigorously to expand the industrial base of the country by encouraging private sector industrial projects and by initiating the development of large-scale industrial projects in the public sector. The government's motives for promoting industrial expansion include:

- The desire to exploit Saudi Arabia's natural resources in as efficient (and profitable) a way as possible. Thus, large public-sector projects and joint ventures draw on crude petroleum and natural gas (much of which used to be flared) as raw materials. An added advantage of this form of industrial development is that it increases the vertical integration of the newly Saudiized domestic oil industry, giving it more clout world-wide.

- The desire to diversify the economy. It is recognized that petrochemical and other energy-related projects contribute little in this respect, insofar as their performance is strongly related to demand conditions in the international energy markets. Light industries, which are the domain of the private sector, are more useful in increasing the level of economic diversification, although the scope for their expansion is limited.
- The desire to ensure a greater degree of regional balance, by positioning industries in a number of different localities so as to provide employment for underemployed labor, distribute the Kingdom's wealth more widely, and consolidate the Kingdom's physical infrastructure.
- The desire to enhance the role of the private sector, especially as the public sector continues to expand. Light industries are regarded as an eminently suitable avenue for the utilization of private capital.
- The desire to offer local banks the opportunity to assume a greater degree of sovereign risk, to ensure the integration of the financial sector into the mainstream of domestic economic activity.

6.3 PROBLEMS AND CONSTRAINTS. Saudi Arabia's plans for industrial expansion, while ambitious, have a limited opportunity for achieving the objectives outlined above. The problems facing the industrial sector in Saudi Arabia are unusual for a developing country, where the typical pattern is abundant labor, underdeveloped natural resources, and capital and foreign exchange scarcity. In Saudi Arabia, labor is in short supply, one natural resource (petroleum and its by-products, mainly natural gas) is highly developed, and neither capital nor foreign-exchange constraints are binding in a serious sense.

The problems and constraints facing the Kingdom's industrial development schemes can be detailed as follows:

- The Kingdom's most ambitious industrial objective, to become an international force in the production and marketing of petrochemicals, is almost sure to involve it in disputes with its trading partners in western Europe and the United States. The market for petrochemicals is currently depressed, and the anticipated $3 billion (or more) worth of petrochemicals that Saudi Arabia is expected to be producing when all petrochemical projects are onstream will require that the Kingdom fight for a major share of the international market. The EEC and the United States are likely to intensify the degree of protectionism currently in effect to protect their petrochemical industries, citing as pretext the heavy subsidization of feedstock in Saudi Arabia (where the government charges producers $0.50 per million BTU, compared with $4.50-5.00 in western Europe and $3.30-3.50 in the United States.

– Regardless of how emphatic Saudi planners are about promoting private sector participation, the Saudi economy is largely driven by government expenditure, the level of which is to some extent (not totally) dependent on the level of oil revenues, which fluctuate as oil prices vary and Saudi Arabia accommodates OPEC by acting as a swing producer. This results in complications for the industrial sector inasmuch as:

  o The heavy and petrochemical industrial projects require considerable capital allocations, and their scale cannot easily be adjusted up or down. As fiscal pressures intensified and planners became aware that they could not count on nearly infinite supplies of capital, they became more reticent about investing in industrial "megaprojects," cancelling some which had already been planned and slowing down payments on others. This tends to shake the confidence of foreign partners, and complicates marketing plans.
  o Private sector (mostly light) industries are sensitive to the level of government spending, since government-funded or supported projects provide the basis for demand for many light industrial products. By the end of 1983, for instance, ten private-sector factories had closed, and some forty enterprises were reporting serious problems in meeting financial obligations or launching marketing campaigns.

– As in nearly all sectors of the economy, the manpower shortage is a serious constraint. Not only does the scarcity of skilled and unskilled workers translate into high labor costs, but the adoption and implementation of proper management and marketing techniques in the industrial sector is sometimes hampered by the lack of adequate expertise. University education at home and abroad is slowly filling the upper echelons of managements with well-trained Saudis, but the prospects for filling middle management positions with qualified Saudis are problematic.

- Despite modest success in building industrial estates outside of the major industrial centers of Jeddah, Riyadh, Dammam, Yanbu and Jubayl (e.g. partially completed industrial centers in the Qassim province northwest of Riyadh, at Hasa in the Eastern Province and at Mecca), the prospects for additional industrial expansion in the provinces are limited. The need for budgetary austerity necessitates the rethinking of spending priorities, a process likely to penalize projected investment in localities distant from major market outlets and requiring substantial infrastructural investment. While additional estates are planned at Asir, Medina, Hail and Tabuk, earlier projections of provincial industrial growth are being scaled down in size and geographic scope.
- The domestic market is too small to absorb enough production to make economies of scale a factor in most cases. The prospects for foreign markets for Saudi products are limited, and the possibility of GCC integration expanding the scope for Saudi industrial output is circumscribed by the lack of coordination and duplication in industrial effort among GCC members. In this regard, Saudi Arabia is favored. Crude (a primary factor of industrial production) is produced more cheaply and on a larger scale in Saudi Arabia than elsewhere. At the same time, Saudi Arabia has a far larger population than other GCC countries. Gains from integration (in terms of generating demand for locally produced goods) may accrue to other GCC countries – initially, at least.

6.4 INCENTIVES FOR PRIVATE SECTOR INVESTMENT. The private sector is strongly encouraged to participate in industrial development schemes, this being one of the major objectives behind the Kingdom's industrial development strategy. Among the incentives provided to the private sector are:

- exemption from import taxes on imported machinery, spare parts, and raw materials;
- protective tariffs or quotas against competing imports;

- financial assistance on very easy terms (primarily through SIDF financing);
- long-term leasing of industrial sites at nominal rents ($0.03 a sq m for building lands);
- electricity at heavily subsidized rates ($0.02 per KWH, although it appears likely that the cost will have to be increased in line with "rationalization" policies);
- preferential treatment for locally manufactured goods in government procurement;
- assistance in the identification of viable projects through market research and feasibility studies; and
- cheap feedstock and guaranteed supplies of crude for 15-20 years (500 b/d for every $1 billion in investment, although the government is reported to be reneging on some agreements, and in some cases, the "cheap" price was set when oil prices were at a peak, making the terms far less tempting in today's market).

6.5 EXISTING INDUSTRIES. The General Petroleum and Mineral Organization (Petromin) is responsible for the development of the country's oil and mineral resources. The Saudi Basic Industries Corporation (SABIC), set up in 1976, is in charge of the development of basic industries not directly related to petroleum, although it handles some major petrochemical projects.

SABIC seeks to attract funds or joint ventures in which the government is a partner with the private investor. By 1985, SABIC's ten leading heavy industries will be in operation. Three SABIC projects started production in 1983: the Saudi Iron and Steel Company (Hadded), the Saudi Methanol Company (Al-Razi), and al-Jubayl Ferltilizer Company (Samad). Local private firms are encouraged to participate in SABIC-sponsored companies. The National Gases Company (NGC), due to open this year, is the first SABIC venture with the domestic private sector. At the end of 1983, SABIC announced that 20 percent of its share capital of SR 10 billion ($2.87 billion) will be offered to the public starting in early 1984, to be allocated 90 percent to Saudi citizens and 10 percent to GCC citizens, the maximum subscription to any one individual being 1,000 shares (SR 1 million [$284,500]). This established SABIC as the first joint-stock company with Saudi as well as other GCC stockholders – a major, if as yet modest, step toward financial and industrial integration.

The Saudi Industrial Development Fund (SIDF), funded by the Ministry of Finance and National Economy, was set up in 1974 to provide financing for industrial projects.

Its total allocation was increased from $1.8 billion to $3 billion under the Third Plan. As of the first quarter of 1984, the SIDF had approved 906 loans to privately owned companies, its commmitments to date totalling SR 11 billion ($3.13 billion), 97 loans (totalling SR 1.6 billion [$455.2 million]) having been approved in fiscal 1982/83. The chemical sector has been the fastest-growing among the non-energy industries backed by SIDF, accounting for 24 percent of total disbursements – a reflection of downstream offshoot activities ensuing from rapid petrochemical developments. Other sectors benefiting from SIDF support include consumer products and engineering, but construction projects, previously a significant beneficiary, are now being discouraged – a result of the depressed market for construction services. SIDF has lent considerable support to joint venture projects, its total disbursements amounting to SR 4.1 billion ($1.17 billion).

A new Saudi joint stock entity is in the process of being established by royal decree to promote industrial projects: the National Industrialization Company (NIC) of Saudi Arabia, set up in 1983 with a capital of SR 600 million ($170.7 million) by 119 businessmen and firms, four public organizations and three banks. Its role is seen as complementary to SABIC and Petromin; it represents a state-supported joint effort of the business and financial sectors to promote industrialization. Its objectives have been outlined as follows:

- To establish petrochemical, chemical, engineering, and other complementary industries;
- To develop an indigenous industrial administration;
- To promote technology transfers; and
- To cement cooperation between the industrial and commercial sectors

Initial investments in industrial projects by NIC are expected to exceed SR 10 billion ($2.85 billion). Its role is to be further elucidated in the Fourth Plan (1985-90).

7
MANPOWER

7.1 SERIOUS SHORTAGES. The severe shortage of manpower, skilled and unskilled, is by far the most serious obstacle impeding economic development in most oil producing countries in the Gulf region. Saudi Arabia is no exception.

From a development perspective, the manpower issue is not only one of numbers of skilled workers available in various industries, but also one of their general attitudes toward work, their industriousness and entrepreneurial mentality, and their basic motivation to initiate and develop business projects. None of these issues are uniquely Saudi Arabian; they are major problems in any less developed economy. However, in Saudi Arabia, as well as in other oil-exporting countries, they are given more attention because some of the more concrete development problems, such as financing and the availability of capital and international reserves, are nonexistent.

A particularly serious problem is the Saudi obsession with management careers, which are lucrative and offer the best opportunities for advancement. These tend to attract the bulk of the educated male population, the result being unbalanced manpower development, with critically needed skills categories (notably computer, agronomical and engineering skills) being shunned by native Saudis.

7.2 FOREIGN WORKERS. The rapid growth of the Saudi economy and the severe shortage of manpower combine to produce a large percentage of foreigners in the workforce. The official Ministry of Planning tally of foreign workers is 1 million (in an indigenous population of at most 7.4 million), but independent estimates exceed 1.7 million. The total foreign population (including some non-workers) was reliably estimated at 2.2 million in 1980, suggesting that Saudi Arabia has the largest expatriate population in the Gulf in terms of absolute numbers.

There has been a considerable increase in the proportion and number of foreign inhabitants from 1975 to 1980 – a reflection of the rapid population growth rate and the increasing need to rely on foreign manpower. The number of foreigners inhabiting the Kingdom is believed to have more than doubled in those five years. Meanwhile, the proportion of Asians increased at the expense of (non-Saudi) Arabs, Europeans, and Americans. In 1975, only 8.1 percent of the foreign population was believed to be Asian, while 81.7 percent was believed to be Arab, all other groups accounting for the remaining 10.2 percent. By 1980, it is estimated that the proportion of Asians had risen to 35.9 percent, while that of Arabs had fallen to 57.3 percent and other groups to 6.8 percent. This is probably the result of three factors:

- Asian workers were deliberately favored over Arabs because of their reputed docility.
- Asian workers are cheaper in certain employment categories, notably construction and service related jobs, a reflection of excess manpower supply in their countries of origin. Wage surveys indicate that Asians receive lower wages than other foreigners for the same jobs.
- By 1975, certain categories of employment which necessitated knowledge of Arabic (teaching and civil administration) had been largely filled; the greatest scope for expansion was in construction, industry and service-related jobs, for which knowledge of Arabic was not a prerequisite.

Expatriates represent a much higher proportion of the workforce than they do of the population, because a larger proportion of foreigners is economically active. An official survey conducted by the Ministry of Planning in 1980 suggests that about 50 percent of the labor force (1 million out of a workforce of 2.5 million) is foreign. This contradicts the findings of the Ministry of Labor, which listed the number of foreign workers as follows:

Foreign Workers in Saudi Arabia

Country	Number of Workers
North Yemen	600,000
Egypt	250,000
Pakistan	200,000
South Korea	80,000
Philippines	70,000
UK and USA (combined)	25,000-30,000

Source: Labor Ministry Estimate, 1980

The total figure for the above countries (which are not the only labor exporters) is clearly in excess of 1 million, suggesting a deliberate underestimate by the Ministry of Planning.

Expatriate manpower is concentrated mainly in the industrial and construction sectors; the service and trade sectors are manned more heavily by Saudi nationals.

The large percentage of foreign workers poses a number of very serious problems, notably:

- It contributes to social tensions, especially in a country as socially conservative as Saudi Arabia.
- It sometimes results in ethnic and religious tensions. Although Muslim workers are favored over non-Muslim ones (note the large number of Pakistanis and the growing number of Turks), there are large non-Muslim groups. Filipinos (in Saudi Arabia nearly all are Christian) have been particularly problematic because of the belief that Muslims are not well-treated by the Christian majority in the Philippines. The relatively large population of Lebanese Christians in Saudi Arabia is among the best adapted, with many of its members occupying influential positions.

From the point of view of the labor-exporting countries, exporting workers to Saudi Arabia has definite advantages: it creates employment opportunities for otherwise unemployable workers, and generates foreign exchange through the remittances sent home (1982 estimate: SR 14.4 billion [$4.19 billion]). However, the loss of skilled labor is a serious problem; labor migration creates shortages in certain employment categories in the labor-exporting countries. At same time, these workers usually have no opportunity of settling permanently in Saudi Arabia (much less becoming naturalized); they almost invariably return home after many years' absence, the result being a two-tiered economy with the returning workers constituting a class far wealthier than average, with attendant social and cultural tensions.

7.3 TREATMENT OF FOREIGNERS. Foreign workers living in the city of Dhahran, which is operated by ARAMCO, are to a large extent shielded from the puritanical exigencies of Saudi society. Generally speaking, most foreign workers are now adequately housed, this having been achieved in the course of the implementation of the Second Plan. Like other Gulf countries, Saudi Arabia has tough immigration laws. While naturalization is not entirely impossible for

Muslim Arabs, foreigners require visas to enter and often to leave the country. They may not always be allowed to bring their families with them. They are not permitted to change jobs without the written consent of their current employers, a regulation calculated to restrict their mobility. Furthermore, the government's highly publicized determination to reduce dependence on foreign labor creates a feeling of insecurity among many, if not all, foreign workers.

Illegal immigration is a common phenomenon in Saudi Arabia, as a result of the impossibility of properly counting (or, for that matter, controlling) the number of foreign workers in the country. The borders are next to impossible to control; there are huge tracts of uninhabited land which make it fairly easy to enter the country illegally. Another complicating factor is the influx of a large number of foreigners during the pilgrimage season (853,555 in 1982), not all of them legitimate pilgrims. Local employers do not, for the most part, exhibit any reluctance to hire illegal immigrants. The wage rate for illegals is, naturally, lower than average.

7.4 TRAINING PROGRAMS. The Third Development Plan (1980-85) placed special emphasis on education and vocational training. Certain organizations, like the Organization for Technical Education and Vocational Training, were recently established to promote manpower training programs. More than 30 vocational training centers have been set up, with an average of 6,000 skilled workers graduating yearly, the best of whom are sent by the government for additional training in the United States, Germany, France and the United Kingdom. An estimated 35,000 students will have graduated from vocational training centers by 1985.

University education has been successfully used to train graduates for the hydrocarbon industries. In many cases, however, vocational training is a more efficient (and speedier) way of producing workers with the needed skills. Public sector industrial projects are often accompanied by human resource development centers to train indigenous workers. At the Jubayl industrial complex, it was considered desirable to set up a centralized human resource development center to supply the burgeoning industries with trained labor (rather than conducting separate training programs for each individual industry). The experiment has proved less than successful, leading to postponement of a similar center that had been projected for the Yanbu industrial complex.

With pressure on foreign companies to "Saudiize" their workforce whenever possible and greater Saudi insistence on manpower development schemes as an integral part of projects executed by foreign firms, more foreign firms are setting up their own training programs. At the same time, nationally-owned industries (including many recently Saudiized financial institutions) assign high priority to training indigenous manpower. A number of approaches have been attempted; those focusing on classroom-type instruction have generally produced disappointing results. In most instances, a modular approach (alternating on-the-job training with classroom sessions) is the most fruitful, as it offers an immediate opportunity for practical application of newly-developed skills. In some cases, especially those involving the transfer of advanced technological skills, a structured on-the-job training is preferable.

As the training function is at present largely fulfilled by foreigners, a number of problems typically plague the training process, regardless of the approach selected. These involve language problems, and sociocultural differences in attitudes to education which foreign instructors are sometimes slow to grasp.

Some firms operate highly successful training centers to which workers from other companies may be admitted upon payment of a fee. Other firms do not operate on a large enough scale (or work on projects with a long enough span) to justify the expense of an in-house training program; these usually find it necessary to rely on outside trainers.

Foreign firms, like West Germany's GTZ and the U.S.-based Vokatron, participate and assist in training programs and have played in important role in this area. Vokatron is particularly active; by 1985, it should have ten vocational centers, three on-the-job training centers, and four mobile training centers in operation. While plans for manpower training are ambitious, much will depend on the willingness of Saudis to make use of available opportunities.

7.5 THE ROLE OF WOMEN. Saudi women play a highly restricted role in the economic life of the Kingdom. This can be atttibuted to;

- Puritanical attitudes which frown upon the employment of women – not because of any religious injunction against such employment, but rather because of the desire to maintain strict segregation of the sexes. As a result, employment opportunities exist for women primarily (in fact, almost exclusively) in the areas of education and medicine, where they interact mostly with other females.

- Saudi women do not, in many cases, seem very eager to work, although many of them are eager to receive an education. In the absence of economic pressures on the family (there is rarely a need for both spouses to work), there is a tendency to view work as demeaning to a woman's dignity, not to say an advertisement of the family's failure to live comfortably on the husband's income. Thus, only the most highly motivated women seek employment.

Women accounted for 5.9 percent of total civilian employment in 1979/80, with Saudi women constituting 7.2 percent of the Saudi segment of the workforce. The number of employed women is projected by the Third Development Plan to increase from 147,900 in 1979/80 to 164,900 (a 2.2 percent increase), with the number of Saudi women in the labor force increasing from 103,000 to 120,000 (a 17 percent increase).

The failure to make use of Saudi women in the labor force is a major impediment to the government's efforts to reduce dependence on foreign workers. Moreover, it is recognized even by Saudi planners as a waste of resources, since much is spent on the education of women. The new Five Year Plan has explicitly stated the government's intention to provide education to all children (male and female) and to seek to develop employment opportunities for women "in a manner which would not be contrary to Islam."

7.6 DISTRIBUTION OF EMPLOYMENT BY SECTOR. The oil sector is by far the most productive in Saudi Arabia, and offers the highest wages. The very fact of its high productivity, however, means that its labor needs are minimal, so that it employed no more than 1.5 percent of the working population in 1979/80.

Agriculture is the largest employer, accounting for 24.2 percent of employment in 1979/80. This reflects the traditional role the agricultural sector has played in Saudi society; nonetheless, the number of workers in the agricultural sector and the proportion of the total workforce that sector employs have both been shrinking (the percentage of the labor force in agriculture had been 39.8 in 1974/75).

Employment in community and social services more than doubled from 1974/75 to 1979/80, to the point where it is the second largest employer, accounting for 19.5 percent of total employment in 1979/80. Employment in construction doubled in absolute terms, and the construction sector was a major employer in 1979/80, accounting for 13.3 percent of total employment, although the percentage is expected to drop as the construction sector is adjusts to a lower level of economic activity.

Trade, a highly lucrative occupation in a growing, prosperous and economically open society, has increased its share of the workforce from 8.8 percent in 1974/75 to 12.6 percent in 1979/80, a consequence of rapid economic growth. The government sector absorbed more workers over the period of the Second Five Year Plan, but the percentage of workers it employed dropped from 14.0 to 13.0, a reflection of government reluctance to expand the role of the public sector. Transportation increased its share (from 6.5 percent to 8.7 percent) as infrastructural improvements and the growth of the national airline, Saudia, increased employment opportunities in that sector.

The manufacturing sector continued to employ the same percentage (4.2) of the labor force. Mining and utilities increased both the absolute number of workers they employ and the percentage of the workforce they employ, but remain of limited importance as employers.

7.7 PROSPECTS. The manpower sector is likely to undergo considerable changes as the government presses ahead with its Saudiization efforts. The most likely developments for manpower in the next few years are:

- More emphasis will be placed on vocational training, with students channelled toward vocational training programs rather universities.
- Better career planning and counseling will be made available to Saudis at an early stage, proabably at the secondary level of education.
- In university and vocational training programs, special emphasis will be placed on critically needed skills. At the university level, computer, agricultural and engineering expertise will be emphasized. At the vocational training levels, high-technology skills and skills suitable for private and public sector manufacturing ndustries will be stressed.
- Adult-education and anti-illiteracy programs will be

pushed aggressively, both for social reasons and as a means to equip more Saudis for jobs.

- The role of women is not likely to be expanded greatly, although women will continue to make progress in certain professions – notably, where they can avoid interacting with men.

8
FINANCE SECTOR

8.1 DECELERATION IN THE MONEY SUPPLY. Monetary expansion has become a way of life in Saudi Arabia. During the six-year period between 1973 and 1979, the money supply increased at a compounded annual average rate of approximately 48 percent per year.

A major deceleration in the growth rate of the money supply occurred in 1978 and 1979. In 1978, the money supply grew by 28 percent compared with its 58 percent growth in 1977; in 1979, it grew by only 11 percent. The deceleration in monetary expansion has helped reduce the rate of inflation; consumer prices fell 1.6 percent in 1978, and increased by 1.9 percent in 1979.

By 1980, increasing oil revenue was causing government expenditures to accelerate at such a rate that the money supply could only resume its rapid growth. In 1980, money and quasi-money increased by a full 17.4 percent, only to grow further in 1981 by a whopping 33.0 percent. The rapid monetary expansion continued in to 1982, when the monetary growth rate was 20.2 percent. In the first quarter of 1983, a more restrictive mood at the Saudi Arabian Monetary Agency (SAMA, the Saudi Central Bank), coupled with vastly reduced economic expectations (a result of falling oil revenues and the Gulf War), and the concurrent reduction in the growth of government spending caused quasi-money to contract, and the total figure for the money supply to register a growth rate of no more than 8.4 percent on an annual basis. In the second quarter of 1983 the money supply grew only slightly (7.8 in the second and third quarters of 1983, and it did not change at all in the third quarter of 1983.

Consumer prices did not echo monetary growth during that period, largely because of heavy government subsidization of consumer goods, and also the importance of imports, the price of which did not generally increase at a very rapid rate, and this at a time when the Saudi Riyal maintained its value and even appreciated slgithly. Inflation was estimated at 3.7 percent in 1980 despite the rapid rate of monetary growth, 2.7 percent in 1981, and about 1.0 percent in 1982. It is believed to have accelerated slightly in the first quarter of 1983, only to become (slightly) negative in the second and third quarters, a reflection of monetary deceleration and continued subsidization.

It should be noted, however, that the figures for the money supply in Saudi Arabia do not tell the whole story, as there are many unofficial and invisible agents (such as money changers, whose transactions cannot be monitored effectively) who play a very important role but whose activities are not taken into account in the calculation of the monetary aggregates. In fact, the Saudi monetary authorities have recently taken steps to limit the scope of activities of money changers.

8.2 THE SAUDI ARABIAN MONETARY AGENCY. The Saudi Arabian Monetary Agency (SAMA), under the control of the Ministry of Finance, acts as a central bank, its avowed aims being a predictable riyal, a higher level of private investment, a good domestic liquidity situation, price stability, and growth of the non-oil sector. The monetary control SAMA exercises is especially important in view of the virtual absence of taxes, which severely limits the scope of fiscal policy. At the same time, SAMA did not, until very recently, act very forcefully as monetary authority. This was attributed to a variety of factors, namely:

- Money changers account for an estimated 25 percent of funds. Their activities have been largely unregulated, making it nearly impossible to exercise effective control over the money supply.
- SAMA has no discount window or swap facility to act a lender to banks, its only means of boosting domestic liquidity during tight periods being the discreet placement of funds with banks on behalf of government agencies, as it did in 1979, 1980 and 1981.
- Interest rates are subject to no limits. In line with the Kingdom's Islamic legislation, interest rates on loans or deposits are referred to as "commissions." Thus defined, they are disguised as accounting items, which precludes their designation as usurious, and so shields them from government control.
- "Jawboning" and moral suasion are a preferred way of controlling the financial sector. SAMA is known to have resorted to such informal controls to curb interst rates or bank credit growing at an excessively

rapid rate. The system works fairly well, largely because thge financial community is small and closely-knit, but this arrangement increases the uncertainty of monetary policies, particularly as regards the speed of implementation.

- Given the prevalence of "megaprojects" with enormous financing needs, regulations limiting bank lending to one borrower to no more than 25 percent of capital have proved difficult to enforce.

There are signs, however, that SAMA will be acting more forcefully. These include:

- In 1981, money changers were required to register with SAMA and to cease acting as lenders and deposit-takers. Further restrictions (including capital and reserve requirements) are being introduced, to go into effect in December, 1984.
- In February 1984, SAMA issued SR 350 million ($99.57 million) of banking security deposits. These are 91-day deposits, similar to government securities, and while the size of the issue is small and there is no secondary market for the securities (although redemption before maturity is a possibility), the introduction of such securities is regarded as heralding the birth of a domestic money market, which could lead to more effective SAMA control of the financial sector.
- SAMA is becoming more serious about limitations on borrowing as a percentage of bank capital. This is evidenced by a circular in late 1983 requiring letter of credits to be counted toward the 25 percent maximum, and refusal to relax the ceiling in a number of recent instances, causing some financing to have recourse to two syndications.
- SAMA has become quite emphatic about limiting the internationalization of the riyal. The market for offshore riyals had been growing at a rapid rate through 1982, a reflection of growing financial sophistication, and a desire (especially on the part of foreign contractors and large corporate borrowers) to spread risks. By 1983, the combined value of riyal syndicated loans was estimated at SR 4.500 billion ($3.2 billion). SAMA intoduced a circular in January, 1983, requiring local banks to obtain advance authorization for:

  o Inviting foreign banks to participate in riyal-denominated syndications.

- o Participating in offshore riyal facilities .
- o Joining foreign-currency syndicated facilities for non-residents.

The result was tighter control of riyal syndications (to the detriment of offshore banks based in Bahrain), and a greater degree of SAMA control over the supply of riyal-denominated credit. The effectiveness of the SAMA decree was, however, limited by the fact that the syndication market is at present extremely thin (with the slowdown of economic activity), so that there is considerable slackness in the financial sector.

8.3 COMMERCIAL BANKS. Ten commercial banks are authorized to operate in Saudi Arabia. Of these, two (the National Commercial Bank and Riyadh Bank Limited, by far the two largest banks) are wholly Saudi-owned. The other banks, originally foreign-owned, were required by a 1977 decree to sell a majority of their shares to Saudi nationals or entities. The process of "Saudi-ization" of banks operating in Saudi Arabia is now complete.

Total bank capital and reserves increased by 7.2 percent to SR 10.86 billion in 1982/83, a far lower growth rate than the 36.7 percent recorded in the previous fiscal year, which reflects the impact of tighter monetary policy and slower economic growth. The growth that did occur is a reflection of the higher level of deposits (demand deposits increased by 12.1 percent in 1982/83, time and savings deposits by 10.2 percent, and other deposits by 11 percent), which in turn is probably a reflection of the increased number of bank branches (eighty-four new branches were opened in 1982/83, bringing the total throughout the Kingdom to 450). The growth of deposits, it should be noted, was nonetheless lower in 1982/83 than in the previous year (when demand deposits grew by 23.9 percent, time and savings deposits by 31.9 percent and other deposits by 52 percent). The use of checks continued to increase, as bank clearings increased by 29 percent in 1982/83.

On the asset side, the growth of loans to the private sector declined more steeply than the growth of deposits: from 15.7 percent in 1981/82 to 6.12 percent in 1982/83, a reflection of the slowdown in economic activity. It is expected, however, than the demand for commercial bank loans will increase this year, as tighter liquidity increases the pressure on the private sector. Foreign assets grew impressively in 1982/83 (by 23.2 percent), despite evident SAMA aversion to the movement of funds abroad (primarily to the offshore market in Bahrain), evidenced by taxes imposed by SAMA on interest earned by banks from offshore lending.

8.4 BANK CREDIT. As mentioned above, the total volume of commercial bank loans to the private sector increased at a reduced rate in 1982/83. There was no dramatic shift in credit allocation by sector in that fiscal year: the commerce sector continued to be the largest recipient of bank credit (34.7 percent of total, compared with 36.9 percent in the previous year), followed by the construction sector (22.5 percent of total, compared with 21.3 percent in the previous year), whose credit needs increased with the slowdown in payments on government contracts. Perhaps the most intersting development was the more than doubling of the small share of transport and communication (from 2.5 percent in 1981/82 to 5.3 percent in 1982/83).

A principal source of borrowing for a creditworthy corporation is overdrafts. Saudi riyal interst rates fell in January 1983, but climbed steadily thereafter as a result of tightening liquidity and the consequent increased demand. It is projected to peak at 11 percent in 1984 before softening somewhat. Fluctuations in the volume of private sector borrowing and interest rates are generally caused by:

- Liquidity considerations. These are represented by the following factors:

  - o The timing of major disbursements by the government, particularly payments for large contracts and land compensation.
  - o The rate of capital outflows, which in turn reflects anxiety about regional and domestic political conditions.
  - o The prevailing Eurodollar interest rate.

- Certain religious occasions (like the holy month Ramadan), during which consumer spending is high and government payments are exceedingly slow, resulting in tight liquidity.
- Seasonal variations reflecting budget-related pressures; as in many countries, the pre-budgetary period (first quarter of the solar year) is among the tightest in terms of credit.

8.5 OTHER FINANCIAL INSTITUTIONS. The only financial intermediaries of note other than commercial banks (and money changers) are investment banks, represented by the Saudi Investment Bank Corporation (SIBC), which is 65 percent Saudi-owned, the major foreign stockholder being Chase Manhattan.

SIBC finances agricultural, industrial and commercial enterprises through lending and equity investments.

No development banks, mortgage banks or savings banks in the proper sense of the word operate in Saudi Arabia. Pension funds and insurance companies do not act as financial intermediaries, insofar as they do not loan money to corporations. Development funds are, however, important sources of capital financing. Five of these are currently in operation, namely:

- The Saudi Industrial Development Fund, established in 1974
- The Saudi Agricultural Bank, established in 1966
- The Public Investment Fund, established in 1971, provides interest-free loans to priority projects. (Disbursement, split equally between SABIC and Petromin projects, totalled SR 18 billion in 1983).
- Real Estate Development Fund, established in 1974.
- The Credit Fund for Contractors, etablished in 1974, to grant interest-free loans to Saudi contractors.

No stock or bond market exists in Saudi Arabia. Plans to establish a stock market were dealt a blow by the financial confusion caused by the collapse of neighboring Kuwait's parallel stock market; nonetheless, the Ministry of Finance announced early this year that a central stock registration conmpany (the Saudi Share Registration Company) is in the process of being formed by Saudi Arabia's commercial banks, to become operational by next year with strict limits on debt financing to discourage overspeculation. At present, sale of shares is negotiated through commercial banks, an example being the sale of SABIC shares to the public early this year.

8.6 ISLAMIC BANKING. An example of how the rigorous code of the Sharia may affect the conduct of business in Saudi Arabia can be found in the practice of Islamic banking. Islamic banks have sprung up in a number of Islamic countries – notably, in the Gulf states, Egypt, the Sudan, and Jordan. Islamic banking is predicated on the premise that fixed interest charges on loaned capital are tantamount to "riba" (literally "excess" or "usurious profit"), which is prohibited by the Sharia. Saudi Arabia has played an instrumental role in devising arrangements for the borrowing of capital to involve proportional, rather than fixed return. This kind of arrangement, which is not unlike a limited partnership or a profit sharing scheme, is the cornerstone of Islamic banking in the sense that the lender is deemed to have "earned" the return on his capital by sharing in the risk, an so does not violate the Sharia. The institution most often invoked in such a contract is the medieval practice of "mudaraba," according to which the borrower's liability is limited in the case of losses being incurred, whereas profits are shared on a proportional basis between the lender and the borrower.

Saudi Arabia has been a pioneer in the field of Islamic banking, perhaps becuase the puritanical Wahhabi code of the Saudis is one of the strictest. The Islamic Development Bank, which was set up in Jeddah in 1975, is an Islamic bank to the extent that its operations are supposed to conform to the Sharia, and furthermore it finances development projects in member nations, all of which have sizeable Muslim populations. The Saudi Prince Muhammad al-Faisal has been one of the major forces behind Islamic banking instructions such as the Faisal Islamic Bank of the Sudan, and the Bahamian based Islamic Investment Company, the scope of whose operations is international.

Another interesting development is "women's banks", bank branches operated exclusively for the use of women so as to permit women free use of banking services wihout infringing upon the prevailing segregation code. The arrangement is said to be gaining favor in a number of localities.

9
CONSTRUCTION

9.1 GENERAL CONDITIONS. The construction sector is among the most important in Saudi Arabia, although its future prospects are rather dim. In 1981/82, construction accounted for 11.1 percent of GDP (at current prices), somewhat higher than its share the prvious fiscal year (9.7 percent). This was primarily a reflection of the considerable increase in government spending in 1980 and 1981. Nonetheless, the construction sector cannot be said to have kept up with the rest of the economy, which grew very fast in the past five years. In 1977/78, the contribution of construction to GDP had been 14.2 percent. That share fell in the two subsequent years, and did not rally until 1980/81.

Construction employs 13.3 percent of the economically active population, making it the second largest employer after agriculture. Many construction workers are foreigners, which is a reflection of the rapid increase of employment in the sector, which necessitated the importation of foreign labor. In the past five years, employment in the construction sector nearly doubled (from 172,000 in 1974/75 to 330,100 in 1979/80).

9.2 GROWTH OF CONSTRUCTION. The rapid growth of the construction sector in the 1970s is a reflection of a number of development to a large extent common to all Gulf oil-exporting states. These include:

- A rapidly growing native population, necessitating more residential construction.
- Increased sedentarization of the nomadic (bedouin) population, increasing residential construction.
- The influx of a large number of expatriates, which contributed to the increased demand for housing.
- The large infrastructural projects (road building, port development, etc.), which drew heavily on construction services.
- The development of the manufacturing sector to absorb

surplus capital, employ resources more productively, and increase diversification. This in turn generated the need for additional construction services to build factories and facilities for production.

The construction boom was fuelled largely by escalating oil revenues, which were responsible for the development outlined above. By the beginning of the eighties, it appeared that the growth of the construction sector had reached its limit, particularly because:

- Oil income was declining as a result of the oil glut, a factor which limited the availability of funds for megaprojects, and encouraged the rethinking of all new projects, as well as a number of existing ones.
- The demand for residential housing was tapering off. The net disbursements of the Real Estate Development Fund (REDF), the specialized lending agency which financed private residential construction through concessional financing, recorded disbursements at a reduced rate of SR 6 billion ($1.80 billion) in 1979/80 (compared to the peak level of SR 8.8 billion [$2.51 billion] in 1976/77). Excess demand in the private housing market had been nearly eliminated, and the importance of residential construction was bound to decline; it accounted for about 10 percent of total construction in 1979/80, compared with over 25 percent five years earlier.
- Many large infrastructural projects had been completed, with little prospect of additional gigantic projects to follow.
- The overall slowdown in the level of economic activity, brought about by government austerity, fears about the Gulf War, and the end of the boom mentality, reduced private sector demand for industrial construction.
- Finally, the monetary authorities' extremely conservative policies regarding liquidity and credit limited the availability of financing for projects which could generate demand for construction services.

9.3 ADVERSE DEVELOPMENTS. Negative signs for the construction sector have been multiplying since early 1982, when fiscal pressures brought about by the oil glut became intense. The adverse developments for the construction sector since that date can be summarized as follows:

- The Saudi budget for 1982/83 was released, projecting the smallest increase in capital spending (the major source of funding for construction projects) in three years.
- The advance payment ceiling for state contracts was halved to 10 percent in the summer of 1982.
- The 1983/84 budget was then released, projecting a depressed level of public spending. Figures indicated an actual decline in public spending for fiscal 1982/83 of 15 percent from the previous fiscal year, and actual disbursements 25 percent lower than their budgeted level.
- Payments to construction companies on state contracts were delayed – by three months in some cases, resulting in serious financial hardship for many companies.
- Strict tendering rules were enacted in March, 1983, requiring government agencies and ministries to advertize all projected schemes and to give all companies a chance to bid. This not only complicated the contracting procedure for new projects; it also led to the cancellation of projects tenders already in effect so that the schemes in question would be put out to public bidding.
- A new rule in early 1983 required all foreign companies to award 30 percent of all state contracts to localy owned entities. This resulted in considerable confusion, particularly about the classfication of joint ventures. The government's attitude appears to have been unrelenting; Commerce Ministry officials have indicated that they will permit only 100-percent Saudi-owned enterprises to qualify for the 30 percent to be awarded.

9.4 CURRENT CONDITIONS AND PROSPECTS. Construction awards have registered declines for every month in 1983 – except for February, when they increased by 14.1 percent. Even this was more than offset by a decline of 18.2 percent in January 1984, the number of awards in that months being slightly less than twice the September 1975 level, a fall of 65.5 percent from the level of January, 1983. The number of awards revived modestly in Feruary but not enough to warrant optimism.

Expenditure on construction (based on the volume of monthly disbursements for building) has fallen over the same period, but not nearly as sharply. It has been falling more or less steadily since January 1983, the

February level being 14.5 percent lower than the figure for February 1983.

The prospects for the construction sector are not necessarily as grim as is generally feared. A number of mitigating factors are in operation. These include:

- A number of overdue projects cannot be postponed any longer. Examples of these are housing projects in Qatif and Ahsa, which was awarded to a French company early this year (having been pending for a year), and a hospital projected for Riyadh that has been recently awarded to a South Korean company, having first been put out to tender as far back as 1982.
- The megaprojects that have already been completed (such as the KKIA, King Khalid International Airport at Riyadh, which opened late last year and cost $3.2 billion to complete) will require considerable maintenance, generating the need for construction company services.
- A number of infrastructural projects (generally smaller in scale than those already completed) are still necessary, in rural areas as well as in cities, while other projects form a necessary sequel to already completed projects. Furthermore, the Saudis have indicated a firm commitment to projects necessary for the infrastructural integration of the Gulf Cooperation Council (GCC) - for instance, a gas grid based on Saudi Arabia's associated gas from offshore fields inthe Eastern province is a distinct possibility.
- Some projects are deemed vital to the national interest in light of the same political and military developments in the Gulf that have contributed to the gloom prevailing in business circles. Such projects are expected to go ahead more or less regardless of fiscal constraints. These include the ambitious underground oil storage facilities at Yanbu on the Red Sea, which is being completed with assistance from Scandinavian, Canadian, British and French companies. Also, defense-related expenditure is likely to continue its massive increase, necessitating the construction of basic (campsites, etc.) and auxiliary (primarily hospital) facilities.

The prospects for the construction sector can be summarized as follows:

- Opportunities for foreign contractors will not disappear. Indeed, they there may be more of these one year from now than today's depressed level of construction activities would suggest.

- There will be more intense competition between construction firms. It will be necessary for foreign companies to devote more resources to the interpretation of Saudi government ordinances. Construction companies will generally have to learn to work with more Saudi partners, and also to expect lower profits.
- Government departments have indicated that they will emphasize quality and cost efficiency and de-emphasize quantity and rapid completion in awarding construction contracts.
- Payments may be disbursed somewhat more rapidly in the future, but it will be essential to obtain financing on flexible terms.
- The Saudis' emphasis on vocational training will continue to manifest itself. Construction company will improve their competitive position if they are able to demonstrate a capability for manpower development and transfer of technology.
- A number of firms previously doing business elsewhere in the Middle East are likely to enter the Saudi market as opportunities dry up in other Middle Eastern countries. Turkish contracting firms have begun to penetrate the Saudi market, and they are making maximum advantage of their familiarity with region and the cultural compatibility of their workers with the native population. Their entry into the market is likely to intensify competition, and cut further into profits, as pressure builds up for lower and lower bids.

10
BALANCE OF PAYMENTS

10.1 EXPORTS. Crude oil and oil products account for nearly all Saudi exports, all other exports (excluding re-exports, which are arbitrarily excluded from the trade balance) amounting to a negligible amount.

Saudi exports increased at an erratic rate during the past decade, reflecting alternately escalating and moderating oil prices. Exports quadrupled in value in 1974. Thereafter exports increased at a moderate rate, from $30 billion in 1974 to $37 billion in 1978. During that period the volume of oil exports fluctuated without any specific trend, so that the movement in export values was no longer a mere reflection of oil prices.

The value of oil exports rose by 57 percent to $57.8 billion in 1979 as prices climbed rapidly that year, and Saudi Arabia increased the volume of oil exports (by 13.5 percent) to accomodate the escalating demand for oil that accompanied the Iranian Revolution. The following year saw even sharper price increases, which, coupled with still higher volume (4.8 percent higher) resulted in a 74 percent increase in the value of oil exports (to $100.6 billion). The increase in oil prices began to taper off in 1981, and the volume of oil exports fell slightly, resulting in a relatively modest increase in the value of oil exports to $109.9 billion In 1982, oil prices began to fall, and Saudi Arabia had to restrict the volume of exports (by 35.4 percent) to reduce the strong downward pressure on prices; as a result, the value of oil exports declined to $72.6 billion.

Complete export figures for 1983 are not available yet, but preliminary figures indicate a steady increase in the volume of oil exports. By the third quarter of 1983, Saudi Arabia was exporting 4.7 mbd, up from 3.35 mbd in the second quarter and 3.18 mbd in the first quarter. The value of total exports in the third quarter of 1983 increased by $3.57 billion to its highest level since the fourth quarter of 1982.

Japan is the largest buyer of Saudi crude, accounting for 23.8 percent of exports in 1982 (up from 17.2 percent in 1981; all of Asia accounted for 43.8 percent in 1982). The EEC accounted for 35.0 percent of Saudi exports (France, the largest European buyer of Saudi crude, and the second largest importer from Saudi Arabia, accounting for 9.0 percent). The United States, the third largest buyer, accounted for 7.8 percent of total exports in 1982 (compared with 13.2 percent in 1981).

10.2 IMPORTS. The of Saudi imports has been growing at a rapid, in some cases phenomenal, rate since the mid-seventies, which is a reflection of:

- A growing native population, augmented further by immigration.
- Greater affluence, generating greater demand for imported consumer items.
- Exposure to foreign cultures and tastes (through the influx of foreigners and Saudis traveling abroad), creating a demand for new consumer items, especially electronic gadgets.
- The impossibility of producing certain items domestically (because of infrastructural, human resource or technological constraints), making import substitution extremely difficult.
- The accrual of massive foreign exchange receipts (from oil exports and foreign investments) to the government, making it a primary source of demand for imported capital goods, as well as various other imported items (notably defense equipment).

Merchandise imports increased from about $2 billion in 1973 to $41.3 billion in 1982. Growth of merchandise imports has occured steadily since the early seventies, although it slowed down in the mid-seventies, as a result of the slower growth rate of government expenditure (to curb inflation) and the congestion of the port system. By the late seventies, port congestion had been effectively eliminated, and government expenditure began growing rapidly with higher oil revenue and the intitiation of the amibtious Second Five Year Plan. In 1980, imports grew by 20.4 percent to $28.3 billion. They grew again by 18.7 percent to $33.6 billion in 1981, and grew even more rapidly in 1982 (by 22.9 percent to $$41.3 billion).

Imports began to decline in 1983; by the third quarter of 1983, they had fallen to their lowest level since the third quarter of 1981.

Major imports include foodstuffs (live animals and animal products, vegetable products, animal and vegetable fats and prepared foodstuffs), machinery, transport equipment, metals, textiles and chemicals.

In 1982, Saudi Arabia's leading suppliers were the United States (21 percent), Japan (19.6 percent), and Germany (11.0 percent). The relative importance of each of these varies from quarter to quarter (Japan overtook the United States in the first and second quarters of 1983, for instance), but, although the order may vary they are usually the three major suppliers.

10.3 CURRENT ACCOUNT. The growth of exports led to the merchandise trade surplus more than doubling in 1980. Import growth nearly offset the more modest growth in exports in 1981, resulting in a slighter larger merchandise trade surplus. The surplus was more than halved, however, in 1982, when falling exports combined with rising imports to reduce it to $31.5 billion. The balance of trade actually recorded a deficit in the first two quarters of 1983, but swang back into surplus ($4.17 billion) in the third quarter of 1983.

The balance on services and transfers (the other component of the current account) has traditionally been in deficit. The major credit (receipt) item in that balance is investment income, which rose steadily (from $4.9 billion in 1979, to $7.4 billion in 1980, $10.9 billion in 1981 and $11.6 billion in 1982. The steady increase in those years is a reflection of the growing volume of Saudi Arabia's international reserves (the trend was, however, reversed last year) and high international interest rates. The debit (payment) items have risen through 1981, as remittances from foreign workers to their home countries (private transfers) increased, tapering off only in 1981, while payments to foreign contractors and consulting firms climbed, as a result of massive development projects, and the rising cost of maintaining the huge stock of accumulated capital.

The current account has tended to act erratically, while generally remaining in surplus (a result of the large surplus in the mechandise balance). The current account surplus increased sharply from $11.1 billion in 1979 to $41.4 billion in 1980 as the merchandise balance surplus increased dramatically. With a more modest growth in the merchandise balance surplus and a growing deficit in the balance on services and transfers, the current account surplus decline to $38.0 in 1981. As the merchandise balance surplus was more than halved and the deficit in the balance on services and transfers declined more modestly, the current account surplus was nearly eliminated in 1982, dropping to $1.3 billion.

10.4 CAPITAL ACCOUNT. The large current account surplus Saudi Arabia registered until last year has made it a major exporter of capital. During the period 1974-81, more than one-third of the accumulated surplus (about $190 billion) was channeled abroad through oil sector transactions, increases in net foreign assets of commercial banks, and private capital movements.

Total official foreign assets (including reserves and other foreign assets) rose by nearly $118 billion during 1974-81. Nearly half of that increase ($62 billion) occurred in 1980 and 1981, when oil export receipts escalated rapidly, and the absorptive capacity of the Saudi economy proved too limited to accomodate more than a fraction of the accruing income. SAMA-held foreign assets were valued at SR 484.22 ($141.2 billion). They shrank somewhat in 1983, as foreign assets had to be drawn down to meet expenses (revenue from oil exports having declined, while import expenses, aid commitments - especially to Iraq - necessitated continued disbursement of foreign exchange). By the third quarter of 1983, foreign assets held by SAMA had fallen to SR 465.71 billion ($135.8 billion).

10.5 FOREIGN AID. Saudi Arabia is a major international aid donor, having an average ratio of aid disbursement to GNP of 6 percent for the years 1976-80, compared to a ratio varying between 0.12 and 0.87 percent for the OECD countries over the same period. While some of the aid disbursed by Saudi Arabia shows strong political biases (Arab and Muslim states are favored, as are states with cool relations with Israel and/or the Soviet Union), Saudi aid is not tied to the purchase of Saudi products or the use of Saudi personnel.

Foreign aid has been regarded by the Saudi government as an instrument of foreign policy. The motives of foreign aid dispensed by the government directly (through bilateral transfers) or indirectly (through donor agencies and multilateral aid organizations) include:

- Extending aid to Arab states threatened by Israel.
- Extending aid to Iraq in its war against Iran.

- Expanding Saudi influence by supporting friendly regimes and buying off anatagonistic regimes in the region.
- Promoting Islamic unity and contributing to the development of the Islamic world, while at the same time insuring that the Islamic concensus remains closer to Saudi Arabia's conception of it than to Iran's or Libya's.
- Gaining prestige and acquiring a favorable image by supporting LDC development.

Official foreign aid is granted on a government-to-government basis. It increased steadily through the past decade from $3.1 billion in 1975 to an estiated $7.0 billion in 1981. Assistance to Muslim states since 1972 totals SR 90 billion (approximately $25 billion), while some SR 2.2 billion ($625 million) was spent on building and renovating mosques and Islamic centers worldwide.

The major Saudi donor agency is the Saudi Fund for Development (SFD). It extends aid to a large number of Arab and non-Arab, Islamic and non-Islamic LDC's in Africa, Asia and South America. By the end of April 1982, SFD had committed $5.4 billion of soft loans ($2.7 billion of which is in grants) for financing 260 development projects in 59 countries. Asian and African countries are the major recipients, accounting for 51 and 48 percent of disbursed funds respectively. The sector that has received the most aid through SFD is transporation (37.6 percent of total), followed by energy (22.2 percent), social infrastructure (15.2 percent), agriculture (14.2 percent), industrial (10.2 percent) and other (0.6 percent).

In addition to SFD, considerable aid is disbursed by Saudi Arabia through mulitlateral organization. These include: the Islamic Development Bank (IDB, headquartered in Jeddah), the OPEC Fund for International Development (OFID) the Arab Bank for Economic Development in Africa (ABEDA), the Arab Fund for Economic and Social Development, the African Development Bank, the World Bank, the International Fund Fund for Agricultural Development, and the International Monetary Fund, to which Saudi Arabia recently agreed to loan $3 billion.

IV. SAUDI ARABIA: STATISTICAL APPENDIX

Table 1.

BASIC INFORMATION

Official Name: Kingdom of Saudi Arabia

Country Abbreviation: SU

Date of Independence: September 23, 1932

National Flag: Green and white with the creed of Islam: "There is no god but Allah; Muhammad is the messenger of Allah," in white Arabic script; beneath the script is a white saber.

National Emblem: Two gold-hilted silver scimitars crossed below the base of a tall palm tree.

Weights and Measures: The metric system prevails.

Time: 3 hours ahead of GMT.

Currency units: Riyal (Rls) = 20 qirsh = 100 hallalas

Languages: Arabic and English

Nature of Government: monarchy

Foreign Policy Position: pro-Western

Area: 2,150,000 sq km (829,997 sq mi)

Selected Climate Parameters:

Riyadh: Average Temperature (C)	
Summer (min-max)	25-42
Winter (min-max)	9-21
Jeddah: Average Temperature (C)	
Summer (min-max)	27-37
Winter (min-max)	20-29

Annual Rainfall: 10.1 mm national average
30.4 mm in Asir

Other: Saudi Arabia suffers from severe duststorms, the southerly kauf and the northwesterly shamal.

Former Kings:	May 1926 - Nov 1953	Abdul Aziz Ibn Saud
	Nov 1953 - Nov 1964	Saud Ibn Abd al-Aziz
	Nov 1964 - March 1975	Faisal Ibn Abd al-Aziz
	March 1975 - June 1982	Khalid Ibn Abd al-Aziz

Membership in Regional Organizations:

Arab Bank for Economic Development in Africa
Arab Fund for Economic and Social Development
Arab Monetary Fund
Co-operation Council for the Arab States of the Gulf
Islamic Development Bank
League of Arab States
OAPEC
Organization of the Islamic Conference

Diplomatic Representation:

U.S. ambassador to Saudi Arabia: Mr. Walter L. Cutler
Saudi Ambassador to the U.S.: Prince Bandar Ibn Sultan
Saudi Ambassador to the UN: Mr. Gaafar M. Allagany

Table 2.

OFFICIAL CALENDAR OF SAUDI ARABIA

	1403 A.H. 1982/83 A.D.	1404 A.H. 1983/84 A.D.
Islamic New Year	17 Oct 1982	6 Oct 1983
Beginning of Saudi Arabian New Year	14 Apr 1983	2 Apr 1984
Ramadan (Fasting Month)	12 June-10 July	31 May-28 June
Eid al-Fitr (Feast at end of Ramadan)	11 July 1983	29 June 1984
Hajj Season (Pilgrimage to Mecca)	23 Aug-21 Oct	14 Aug-12 Sept
Waqfat Arafat (Highlight of Hajj)	16 Sept 1983	5 Sept 1984
Eid al-Adha (Feast of the Sacrifice)	17-20 Sept	6-9 Sept
Saudi Arabian National Day	23 Sept 1983	23 Sept 1984

Note: There are 354 or 355 days per Hijra calendar year.

Source: Businessman's Guide to Saudi Arabia 1983, Ministry of Commerce.

Table 3.

CABINET LIST
(As of December 1983)

Head of State, Prime Minister..................King Fahd Ibn Abd al-Aziz

First Deputy Premier.....................Prince Abdullah Ibn Abd al-Aziz
Second Deputy Premier,
Defense & Aviation Minister..............Prince Sultan Ibn Abd al-Aziz
Foreign Affairs....................................Prince Saud al-Faisal
Agriculture & Water....Abd al-Rahman Ibn Abd al-Aziz Ibn Hasan Al Shaikh
Commerce..................................Sulaiman Abd al-Aziz al-Solaim
Education.........................Abd al-Aziz al-Abdullah al-Khuwaiter
Finance & Economy...............................Muhammad Ali Abalkhail
Health....................................Dr. Abd al-Rahman Al Shaik
Higher Education..........................Hasan Ibn Abdullah al-Shaikh
Industry & Electricity...........................Abd al-Aziz al-Zamil
Information...Ali Hasan al-Shaer
Interior................................Prince Nayef Ibn Abd al-Aziz
Justice......................Ibrahim Ibn Muhammad Ibn Ibrahim Al Shaikh
Labor & Social Affairs.........................Muhammad al-Ali al-Fayez
Municipal & Rural Affairs................Ibrahim Ibn Abdullah al-Angari
Petroleum & Minerals................................Ahmad Zaki Yamani
Pilgrimage Affairs and Awqaf
(Religious Endowments).................Abd al-Wahhab Ahmad Abd al-Wasi
Planning..Hisham Nazer
Communications..........................Hussain Ibrahim al-Mansouri
Transportation..Hussain Mansouri
Posts, Telegraphs & Telecommunications..............Alawi Darwish Kayyal
Public Works & Housing.....................Prince Moutib Ibn Abd al-Aziz
Governor of Makkah........................Prince Majid Ibn Abd al-Aziz

MINISTERS OF STATE

Mohammad Ibrahim Massoud, Mohammad Abd al-Latif al-Milhim, Abdullah Mohammad al-Omran, Omar Abd al-Qader Faqih

Deputy Minister of Interior................Prince Ahmad Ibn Abd al-Aziz
Adviser to Defense & Aviation Minister..........General Othman al-Humaid
President of Youth Welfare........................Prince Faisal Ibn Fahd
Ministers without Portfolio...............Fayez Badr, Abd al-Hadi Taher

DEFENSE

Table 4.

TRADE IN MAJOR CONVENTIONAL ARMS

Supplier	No. Ordered	Weapon Description	Year of Order	Year of Delivery	No. Delivered
France	4	AMX-30 Shahine AAV	1974	(1980)	(2)
				(1981)	(2)
	53	AMX-30-30mm SA AAV	1975	1979	(13)
				1980	(13)
				1981	(13)
				1982	(14)
	359	AMX-30B MBT	1975	1976	(55)
				1977	(55)
				1978	(55)
				1979	(55)
				1980	(55)
				1981	(55)
				(1982)	(29)
	(200)	AS-15TT AShM	1980		
	(24)	AS-365N Hel	1980		
	(48)	Crotale Naval ShAM	1980		
	4	F-2000 Class Frigate	1980		
	(96)	Otomat-2 ShShM	1980		
	(96)	Shahine Landmob SAM	1974	(1980)	(48)
				(1981)	(48)
	2	Durance Class Support Ship	1980		
Italy	200	VCC-1 APC	1982		
Spain	40	C-212A Aviocar Transport	1979		
UK	72	FH-70 155mm TH	1982		
	(40)	Hawk Adv trainer/strike	1981		
	8	SRN-6 Hovercraft	(1980)	1981	(2)
				1982	2

Source: SIPRI Yearbook 1983

TRADE IN MAJOR CONVENTIONAL ARMS

Supplier	No. Ordered	Weapon Description	Year of Order	Year of Delivery	No. Delivered
USA	916	AGM-65A ASM	1979	(1981)	(458)
				(1982)	(458)
	(240)	AIM-7F Sparrow AAM	1978	(1982)	(50)
	1177	AIM-9L AAM	1981	1982	(200)
	(660)	AIM-9P AAM	1979		
	9	As Saddiq Class FAC	1977	1980	(3)
				1981	(4)
				1982	(2)
	1000	BGM-71A TOW ATM	1980	1981	(500)
				1982	(500)
	2010	BGM-71A TOW ATM	1982		
	3	C-130H Hercules Transport	(1981)	1982	3
	5	E-3A Sentry AEW	1981		
	45	F-15A Eagle Fighter/ Interceptor	1978	(1982)	(15)
	2	F-15C Eagle Fighter	1980		
	4	F-5E Tiger-2 Fighter	1982		
	1	F-5F Tiger-2 Trainer	1982		
	6	KC-135 Tanker/Transport	(1981)		
	50	M-110-A1 203mm SPH	(1980)	1981	(25)
				1982	(25)
	18	M-198 155mm TH	1981	(1982)	(18)
	10	RF-5E Tigereye Recce	(1982)		
	(108)	RGM-84A Harpoon ShShM	1977	1980	(36)
				1981	(48)
				1982	(24)
	15	TF-15A Eagle Trainer	1978	1981	6
				(1982)	(9)
	579	V-150 Commando APC	(1980)	1981	(100)
				1982	(100)

Note: Parentheses denote uncertain information

Table 5.

U.S. ARMS TRANSFERS TO SAUDI ARABIA 1973-1982

Combat Aircraft:		
	F-5 E/F Tiger	124+
	F-15 Eagle	47
Airborne Warning & Control:		
	E-3A Sentry	5
Military Transport:		
	C-130 Hercules	25
	KC-130 tanker/transport	6+
Other Aircraft:		28+
Combat Helicopters:		
	AH-1 Cobra gunship	440
Other Helicopters:		6
Missiles:		
	Dragon AT	4,864
	Harpoon anti-ship	196+
	Hawk SA	+
	Maverick AS	3,166+
	Redeye SA	590
	Sidewinder AA	4,166
	Sparrow AA	1,099+
	TOW AT	4,346
Self-propelled Howitzers:		
	M-110 203mm	50
	M-109 155mm	133+
	M-108 105mm	352
Towed Howitzers:		
	M-198 155mm	18
	M-101 105mm	6
Vulcan Anti-Aircraft:		115+
Tanks & Armored Vehicles:		
	M-60 Main Battle	368
	Armored Personnel Carriers	1,329
	Command Post Carriers	156+
	Other Armored Vehicles	433

Note: A plus sign (+) indicates additional but undetermined amounts

Source: MERIP Reports February 1983

Table 6.

SAUDI ARABIA MILITARY PERSONNEL AND EQUIPMENT

Chief of General Staff: Maj-Gen Muhammad al-Salah al-Hammad
Dir-Gen of Public Security Forces: Brig-Gen Abdullah Ibn Al Shaikh
Commander of Land Forces: Maj-Gen Abd al-Muhsin Ali al-Amran
Commander of Air Force: Maj-Gen Muhammad Sabri

Estimated defense expenditure:
1982-1983: SR 92.889 billion ($27.022 billion)
1983-1984: SR 75.733 billion ($21.952 billion)

Military Service: Conscription, males aged 18-35

Total Armed Forces: 51,500

Army: 35,000

2 armed brigades (1 forming)
2 mechanized brigades
2 infantry brigades (1 to be mechanized)
1 airborne brigade (2 parachute battalions, 3 special forces)
1 Royal Guard Regiment (3 battalions)
5 artillery battalions
18 anti-aircraft artillery batterys
18 surface-to-air batterys:
16 with Improved Hawk, 2 with 12 Shahine (48 missiles),
300 AMX-30 and 150 M-60A1 main battle tanks
200 AML-60/-90 armored cars;
350 AMX-10P and 20 VCC-1 with TOW multipleindependently-targetable re-entry vehicles
800 M-113 Panhard M-3 armored personnel carriers
18 M-198 towed and GCT 155 mm self-propelled howitzers
81mm, M-30 107mm mortars
75mm, 90mm, and 106mm recoilless launchers
TOW, Dragon, HOT anti-tank guided weapons
M-163 Vulcan 20 mm, AMX-30SA 30mm, 86 35mm, M-42 40mm self-propelled anti-aircraft guns
Redeye, Shahine, Improved Hawk surface-to-air missiles

(On order: 150 M-60A3 conversion kits; 60 AMX-10P, some 180 VCC-1 TOW mechanized infantry combat vehicles; 200 FH-70 155mm howitzers; some 400 JPz SK-105 self-propelled anti-tank guns; TOW anti-tank guided weapons; Shahine surface-to-air missiles)

Navy: 2,500

2 Fleet HQ
4 PCG-1 corvettes with 2x4 Harpoon surface-to-surface missiles
9 PGG-1 fast attack craft (missile) with 2x2 Harpoon surface-to-surface missiles
1 large patrol craft (ex-U.S. coastguard cutter)
3 Jaguar fast attack craft (torpedo)
MSC-322 coastal minesweepers
4 US landing craft, utility
8 US LCM-6 landing craft, mechanized

(On order: 4 F-2000 frigates, 2 logistic support ships; 2 Atlantic II maritime reconnaissance aircraft; 24 As-365n Dauphine 2 helicopters (4 search and rescue, 20 with air-to-surface missiles); Otomat coast defense surface-to-surface missiles, 200 AS-I5TT air-to-surface missiles.)

Bases: Jeddah (Western Fleet), al-Qatif/Jubayl (Eastern Fleet)
Ras Tanura, Damman Yanbu, Ras al-Mishab.

Air Force: 14,000

170 combat aircraft
3 fighter, ground attack squadrons with 65 F-5E
4 interceptor squadrons:
1 with 15 Lightning F-53, 2 T-55, 3 (1 forming) with 42 F-15
2 operational conversion units with 24 F-5F, 16F-5B, 6 TF-15D
3transport squadrons with 39 C-130E, 25 C-130H, 6 KC-130H,2 Jetstar
2 helicopter squadrons with 12 AB-206B, 14 AB-205, 10 AB-212
Other helicopters: 2 Alouette III, 1 AB-204B, 14 AB-206B, 1 Bell 212, 10 KV- 107IIA.

Trainers: 46 BAC-167, 12 Cessna 172G/H/L.

Air-to-air missiles: Red Top, Firestreak, Sidewinder, AIM-7F Sparrow.
Air-to-surface missiles: Maverick.

(In reserve: 17 Lightning F-53/T-55.)

(On order: 9 F-15, 5 F-5E fighters, 11 TF-15, 1 F-5F trainers, 10 RF-5E reconnaissance, 5 E-3A Sentry airborne warning and control system(AWACS), 1 Boeing 747, 40 C-212-200 transports, 6 Boeing KC-707 tankers, 2 ECM aircraft, 22 AB-212, 8 KV-107 helicopters, 1,000 AIM-7F Sparrow, 1,177 Sidewinder air-to-air missiles, 916 Maverick air-to-surface missiles.)

Para-Military Forces:

National Guard: (25,000)
4 all-arms
16 regular infantry
24 irregular infantry battalions
1 ceremonial cavalry squadron with support units
240 V-150 Commando armored personnel carriers
M-102 105mm howitzers, 81 mm mortars
106mm recoilless launchers, TOW anti-tank guided weapons
20mm Vulcan, 90mm anti-aircraft guns

(On order: 489 Commando including V-300 armored personnel carriers
V-150 self-propelled 20mm anti-aircraft guns
Self-propelled TOW missiles,
90 mm armored fighting vehicles.)

Foreign contract military personnel: 10,000.

Ministry of the Interior:
Counter-terrorist unit with helicopter(s)

Frontier Force and Coast Guard: 8,500
181 coastal, including 12 SRN-6 hovercraft
300 small patrol craft
(On order: 2 SRN hovercraft)

General Civil Defense Administration units

Source: The Military Balance 1983-84

WATER RESOURCES

Table 7.

HIGHLIGHTS OF THE PLAN FOR WATER DEVELOPMENT

Agency	Name of Project	Purpose	Description
Ministry of Agriculture & Water	National Water Plan preparation	Monitor the Rationalization of available water resources	Water allocation and use regulation
	Studies of Wadi Basins Aquifiers & New Water Supply Projects	Data base development and pre-investment studies	
	Dam Construction	Flood protection, aquifier recharge, and water supply	41 existing dams, 5 under construction, 37 new
	Production Well Drilling	Potable and irrigation water	900 total wells
	Expansion of Major Water Supply Systems	Urban/Industrial Potable Water	10 major cities
	Expansion of Small & Medium Water Systems	Urban/Rural Potable Water	315 systems
	O & M of Potable Water Supply	Urban/Rural Potable Water	470 projects

Source: Third Five-Year Development Plan

HIGHLIGHTS OF THE PLAN FOR WATER DEVELOPMENT

Agency	Name of Project	Purpose	Description
(In cooperation with private sector)	Modernization of irrigation systems in rural areas	Irrigated agriculture for food production	
al-Hassa Irrigation & Drainage Authority	O & M and upgrading of traditional irrigation	Irrigated agriculture for food production	Increase area by 3,000 ha
	Agricultural Production & Marketing Studies	Realize food production potential	16,000 ha total area
	Improvement of Management, Training, & other Agricultural Services	Increase efficiency & crop production	
(In cooperation with private sector)	Modernization of traditional irrigation systems	Water & Labor Conservation and increased production	5,000 ha total area

Table 8.

WATER RESOURCES AND DEMAND: 1980 – 2000
(million cu m per year)

	1980	1985	1990	2000
Supply:				
Non-renewable	3,450	3,450	3,450	3,450
Renewable	1,145	1,145	1,145	1,145
Desalinated	63	605	794	1,198
Reclaimed from urban waste	--	140	335	730
Total	**4,658**	**5,340**	**5,724**	**6,523**
Demand:				
Urban & Industrial	552	823	1,211	2,279
Rural	27	28	31	38
Irrigation	1,832	1,873	2,345	3,220
Total	**2,411**	**2,724**	**3,587**	**5,537**
Surplus	**2,247**	**2,616**	**2,137**	**986**

Source: Ministry of Agriculture and Water

DEMOGRAPHIC INFORMATION

Table 9.

BASIC INDICATORS

	1978	1979	1980	1981
Population				
Total (midyear, thousands)	8,259.0	8,606.0	8,960.0	9,305.0
Age Structure (percent)				
0-14 years	45.2	45.4	45.6	45.5
15-64 years	51.9	51.7	51.5	51.6
65 years and older	2.9	2.9	2.9	2.9
Urban Population (percent of total)	63.5	65.2	66.9	68.1
Population Density				
Per Square Kilometer of Total Area	3.8	4.0	4.2	--
Per Square Kilometer of Agricultural Land	9.6	10.0	10.4	--
Demographic Characteristics				
Crude Birth Rate (per thousand)	45.8	45.7	45.6	45.5
Crude Death Rate (per thousand)	14.3	14.0	13.8	13.5
Life Expectancy (years)				
Total	53.2	53.7	54.1	54.6
Male	51.7	52.1	52.6	53.0
Female	54.8	55.3	55.8	56.3
Total Fertility Rate	7.3	7.3	7.3	7.3

Note: There is a variance of more than six million in population estimates for Saudi Arabia.

Source: World Bank, Social Data 1983

Table 10.

POPULATION OF MAJOR CITIES

Main Towns	**Population (1980 estimates)**
Riyadh (royal capital)	1,000,000
Jeddah (diplomatic capital)	1,300,000 (1981)
Mecca	550,000
Taif	300,000
Medina	290,000
Dammam	200,000

Source: EIU Quarterly Economic Review of Saudi Arabia: Annual Supplement 1982

ECONOMY

Table 11.

MAJOR ECONOMIC INDICATORS

Total GDP (1983): $113.27 billion
Average GDP Annual Growth Rate:
1960-70: 9.9%
1970-81: 10.3%

GDP per capita (1982): $15,780

Gross Domestic Investment (GDI - 1981): $37.77 billion
Average GDI Annual Growth Rate:
1960-70: 17.9%
1970-81: 39.2%

Private Consumption (1981): $14.075 billion
Average annual growth rate:
1960-70: 8.7 %
1970-81: 19.0 %

Source: MERI. Data compiled from World Bank 1983 and IMF statistics

Table 12.

COST OF LIVING INDICES: MIDDLE INCOME SAUDIS
(1979=100)

	Weight	**1979**	**1980**	**1981**	**1982**	**1983(I)**
Food & Beverages	32.42	100	106.4	113.3	114.8	115.0
Rent & Utilities	24.93	100	100.1	99.3	92.8	98.9
Clothing	9.2	100	108.6	113.7	118.7	124.5
Household furniture	5.48	100	98.8	100.6	100.5	101.2
Medical Care	2.49	100	100.2	101.1	114.9	111.9
Transportation & Communications	14.28	100	103.3	107.4	111.7	114.0
Entertainment & Education	2.97	100	96.7	95.8	93.5	97.1
Other	8.20	100	102.2	99.3	95.0	100.3
General Index	**100.00**	**100**	**103.3**	**106.2**	**106.2**	**109.0**

Source: Central Department of Statistics, Ministry of Finance & National Economy, 1983

Table 13.

GROSS DOMESTIC PRODUCT BY ECONOMIC ACTIVITY IN CURRENT PRICES
(million SR)

Sector	1978/79	1979/80	1980/81	1981/82
Industries & Products				
1. Agriculture, forestry, and fishing	4,196	4,648	5,572	5,891
2. Mining and quarrying				
a) Crude petroleum and natural gas	131,098	237,218	340,997	323,328
b) Other	1,120	1,361	1,676	1,969
3. Manufacturing				
a) Petroleum refining	7,442	12,828	18,027	13,260
b) Other	5,173	6,467	7,721	9,091
4. Electricity, gas, and water	248	271	339	468
5. Construction	34,764	43,108	50,348	58,181
6. Wholesale and retail trade, restaurants, and hotels	13,912	17,760	21,984	25,064
7. Transport, storage, and communications	12,764	15,749	17,123	19,871
8. Finance, insurance, real estate, & business services				
a) Ownership of dwellings	9,663	10,962	11,973	12,562
b) Other	6,517	7,853	10,352	13,300
9. Community, social, and personal services	4,155	5,260	5,504	6,813
Government Services				
1. Public administration and defense	10,688	13,545	14,437	18,120
2. Other services	8,224	9,839	15,468	18,242
Less: Imputed bank service charges	-2,342	-3,279	-3,607	-3,968
GDP in producers' values	**247,622**	**383,590**	**517,994**	**522,191**
Import duties	1,917	2,217	2,595	2,542
GDP in purchasers' values	**249,539**	**385,807**	**520,589**	**524,733**

Source: Central Department of Statistics, Ministry of Finance

BANKING AND FINANCE

Table 14.

FINANCIAL SURVEY

INTERNATIONAL LIQUIDITY
(million U.S. dollars)

	1979	1980	1981	1982	1983	1984*
Total Reserves Minus Gold	19,273	23,437	32,236	29,549	27,287	25,136
Foreign exchange res.	17,378	20,747	27,998	23,813	17,457	14,280
SDRs	196	271	248	638	510	563
Reserve position in Fund	1,699	2,418	3,990	5,098	9,321	10,292
Gold (mn fine troy ounces)	4.567	4.567	4.567	4.596	4.596	4.596
Gold (national valuation)	211	204	186	177	168	171

MONETARY SURVEY
(billion SR)

	1979	1980	1981	1982	1983+
Foreign Assets (net)	218.18	313.83	484.17	539.25	518.05
Claims on Private Sector	26.73	37.25	43.25	50.16	56.22
Money	54.70	58.96	72.98	83.78	88.53
Quasi-Money	11.28	18.48	30.01	40.01	40.13
Government Deposits (net)	110.98	188.46	335.69	350.43	333.36
Other Items (net)	67.96	85.18	88.74	115.19	112.25
COMMERCIAL BANKS					
Reserves	13.59	8.19	8.27	10.81	9.42
Foreign Assets	18.19	32.23	53.36	61.00	56.43
Claims on Private Sector	26.73	37.25	43.25	50.16	56.20
Demand Deposits	31.00	33.28	43.49	49.34	50.88
Foreign Currency Deposits	1.90	4.65	8.08	10.33	10.38
Foreign Liabilities	7.47	9.15	9.07	5.97	3.22
Government Deposits	.84	3.56	6.80	8.21	7.49
Capital Accounts	2.54	4.15	5.56	7.82	9.22
Other Items	5.39	9.04	9.94	10.61	10.65
SAUDI ARABIAN MONETARY AGENCY					
Foreign Assets	207.46	290.75	439.88	484.22	465.71
Reserves	38.72	34.46	39.20	44.65	45.46
Government deposits	110.36	185.11	329.13	344.19	327.44
Other	58.37	71.18	71.55	95.38	92.81

* first quarter 1984 figures
+ third quarter 1983 figures

Source: International Financial Statistics, July 1984

Table 15.

LEADING SAUDI BANKS AS OF MID-1981

Bank	Capital Base (million SR)	Foreign Shareholder
National Commercial Bank	1,578	---
Riyad Bank	1,357	---
Saudi American Bank	399	Citibank (40%)
Saudi British Bank	370	Hong Kong and Shanghai Banking Corp. (40%)
Saudi Dutch Bank	292	ABN (40%)
Saudi French Bank	284	Banque de l'Indochine et de Suez (40%)
Arab National Bank	270	Arab Bank Ltd (40%)
Saudi Cairo Bank	235	Banque du Caire (40%)
Bank al-Jazira	157	National Bank of Pakistan (35%)
United Saudi Commercial Bank	300	Banque du Liban et d'Outre Mer United Bank Ltd (30%) Bank Melli Iran

Source: Financing Foreign Operations, Saudi Arabia.
Business International Corporation, February 1984.

Table 16.

COMMERCIAL BANK CREDIT BY ECONOMIC SECTOR
(million SR)

	Amount 1980/81	Share (%)	Amount 1981/82	Share (%)
Agriculture and Fishing	304	0.7	421	0.8
Manufacturing and Processing	3,605	8.8	4,885	9.5
Mining and Quarrying	331	0.8	274	0.5
Electricity, Water, Utilities	1,058	2.6	1,186	2.3
Building and Construction	8,714	21.3	11,519	22.5
Commerce	15,143	36.9	17,747	34.7
Transport and Communication	1,017	2.5	2,725	5.3
Finance	917	2.2	774	1.5
Services	1,610	3.9	1,933	3.8
Miscellaneous	8,301	20.2	9,706	19.0
Total	**40,960**	**100.0**	**51,170**	**100.0**

Source: Financing Foreign Operations, Saudi Arabia.
Business International Corporation, February 1984.

Table 17.

COMMERCIAL BANKS' MAJOR ASSETS AND LIABILITIES
(million SR)

	1981	1982	April 1983
Liabilities			
Total Deposits	74,745	95,420	99,117
Demand Deposits	39,064	48,398	51,762
Others	35,682	47,022	47,355
Assets			
Cash	19,703	11,760	10,856
Foreign Assets	48,474	55,689	66,001
Claims	43,148	50,535	49,397
Ratios			
Cash/Deposits	13.0	12.3	11.0
Credit/Deposits	57.7	53.0	49.8
Foreign Assets/Deposits	64.9	58.4	66.6

Source: Saudi Arabian Monetary Agency Statistical Summary, 1983

Table 18.

EXCHANGE RATES
(SR per U.S. dollar)

Year	Rate
1978	3.3150
1979	3.3650
1980	3.3250
1981	3.4150
1982	3.4350
1983	3.4950
1984	
Jan	3.5050
Feb	3.5050
Mar	3.5150
Apr	3.5150
May	3.5150

Source: International Financial Statistics, July 1984

BUDGET AND PLANNING

Table 19.

BUDGET ESTIMATES
(million SR)

	1981/82	1982/83	1983/84
Revenues	**340,000**	**313,400**	**260,000**
Oil Revenues	333,968	270,579	164,496
Other Revenues	6,032	42,821	60,504
From General Reserves	--	--	35,000
Expenditures	**298,000**	**313,400**	**260,000**
Human Resource Development	26,248	31,864	27,791
Transport & Communication	35,343	32,533	24,950
Economic Resource Development	22,679	22,045	13,209
Health & Social Development	13,716	17,010	13,591
Infrastructure Development	14,126	11,705	9,583
Municipal Services	26,292	26,224	19,070
Defence & Security	82,533	92,889	75,733
Public Administration & Other Gov't Spending	43,113	44,586	47,053
Government Lending Institutions	24,850	23,382	20,000
Local Subsidies	9,100	11,162	9,020

Source: Saudi Arabian Monetary Agency Statistical Summary, 1983

Table 20.

BUDGET ALLOCATION BY SECTOR
(million SR)

Fiscal Year	79/80	80/81	81/82	82/83
Council of Ministers & related headings	27,660	39,102	51,068	51,256
Planning	82	86	104	111
Municipal & Rural Affairs	12,224	19,745	26,292	26,224
Public Works & Housing	3,191	5,759	6,444	4,102
Information	1,055	1,443	1,573	1,581
Foreign Affairs	542	736	1,006	1,114
Defense & Aviation	47,060	59,366	65,084	65,880
Interior	9,839	12,963	17,280	21,139
Labor & Social Affairs	4,182	5,732	4,818	5,279
Health	4,177	5,656	6,832	8,951
Education	16,411	21,485	26,132	31,846
Communications	10,779	16,089	19,150	18,568
Finance & National Economy	8,436	11,421	16,014	19,718
Petroleum & Mineral Resources	1,000	1,225	1,294	1,498
Commerce, Industry, & Electricity	4,506	4,658	4,746	8,317
Agriculture & Water	4,169	4,161	3,963	12,371
Pilgrimage & Endowments	1,102	1,308	1,957	1,962
Justice & Religious Affairs	814	1,089	1,224	1,370
Subsidies & transfers	23,029	32,976	43,020	32,113
Total	**160,000**	**245,000**	**298,000**	**313,400**

Source: Saudi Arabian Monetary Agency Statistical Summary, 1983

Table 21.

SAUDI BUDGET 1984-1985
(million SR)

EXPENDITURES BY SECTOR

	Budget 1984/85	Budget 1983/84	% Change on Budget	Actual 1983/84	% Over/ Overspent
Defense & Security	79,900	75,733	+ 5.5	--	--
Public Administration & Gov't Utilities	39,090	47,053	-16.9	40,588	-13.7
Human Resources	27,947	27,791	+ 0.6	24,700	-11.2
Transport & Communications	23,630	24,950	- 5.3	22,190	-11.1
Social Development	18,085	13,591	+33.0	14,140	+ 4.0
Development of Economic Resources	17,560	13,209	+32.9	16,400	+24.2
Municipal Services	17,460	19,070	- 8.4	11,130	-41.6
Lending to Credit Institutions	16,000	20,000	-20.0	16,560	-17.2
Domestic Subsidies	10,525	9,020	+16.7	67,232*	-20.7
Infrastructure	9,830	9,583	+ 2.6	9,380	- 1.0
Total	**260,000**	**260,000**	**0.0**	**222,320**	**-14.5**

*Derived from Official Gov't Figures

Source: Saudi Business, April 16, 1984

ECONOMIC ASSISTANCE

Table 22.

ALLOCATIONS OF SAUDI FOREIGN AID BY COUNTRY

Country	Amount of Aid (million U.S. dollars)
AFRICA	
Algeria	51.46
Botswana	20.64
Burundi	18.83
Cameroon	62.59
Cape Verde	9.85
Chad	30.90
Comoros	28.02
Congo	58.07
Djibouti	27.28
Egypt	215.29
Gabon	51.20
Gambia	14.63
Ghana	38.62
Guinea	89.53
Guinea-Bissau	9.10
Kenya	123.02
Lesotho	4.41
Liberia	20.58
Madagascar	12.36
Mali	145.28
Mauritania	173.58
Mauritius	4.90
Morocco	135.90
Niger	45.52
Rwanda	37.96
Senegal	189.63
Sierra Leone	14.58
Somalia	152.13
Sudan	172.37
Togo	10.26
Tunisia	309.12
Uganda	30.61
Upper Volta	47.11
Zaire	67.20
Zambia	73.00
Zimbabwe	48.83
African Total	**2,547.36**

Source: Saudi Business, April 9, 1984

ALLOCATIONS OF SAUDI FOREIGN AID BY COUNTRY

Country	Amount of Aid (million U.S. dollars)
ASIA	
Bangladesh	211.77
China	205.95
India	133.82
Indonesia	261.41
South Korea	71.73
Malaysia	110.46
Maldives	15.69
Nepal	30.09
Pakistan	237.18
Philippines	20.12
Sri Lanka	98.40
Thailand	51.03
Asian Total	**1,447.65**
MIDDLE EAST	
Bahrain	43.73
Jordan	313.27
Oman	49.47
Syria	260.83
Turkey	244.89
Yemen Arab Republic	145.42
Yemen People's Democratic Republic	34.99
Middle Eastern Total	**1,092.60**
OTHER	
Brazil	56.56
Ecuador	21.28
Malta	51.77
Western Samoa	13.50
Other Total	**143.11**

ENERGY SECTOR

Table 23.

ENERGY OUTLOOK

Crude oil reserves (1984)	166,000,000 bbl
Production (1983)	4,872,000 b/d
Consumption (1983 est incl Neutral Zone)	844,000 b/d
Natural gas reserves (1984)	3,426.72 billion cu m
Natural gas production (1983)	10.80 billion cu m
Finite Reserves:	
Oil	22,600 million toe
Gas	3,088 million toe
Total	25,688 million toe
Installed production capacity (1984) *	12,500,000 b/d
Maximum sustainable capacity (1984)	8,000,000 b/d
Available productive capacity (1984)	8,500,000 b/d
Number of producing wells (1984)	555
Number of refineries (1984)	4
Crude refining capacity	860,000 b/cd
Catalytic reforming capacity	38,000 b/cd

Source: MERI. Data obtained from Petroleum Economist, International Petroleum Encyclopedia, Economist Intelligence Unit Quarterly Reports and Ministry of Oil

Table 24.

ENERGY SUPPLY AND DEMAND
(thousand b/d)

	1978	1979	1980	1981	1982	1983**
Production						
crude oil	8,301	9,532	9,900	9,811	6,473	5,064
oil products	777	835	826	834	851	--
natural gas *	119.82	138.48	148.48	143.50	--	--
Consumption						
oil	285	342	475	577	590	--
natural gas *	26.97	32.03	39.96	69.55	--	--
Exports						
crude oil	7,692	8,818	9,223	9,018	--	8,777
oil products	358	376	407	481	--	--

*million cu m/d
**based on first quarter figures

Sources: OPEC, SAMA, Petroleum Economist

Table 25.

CRUDE OIL PRODUCTION
(million bbl)

Petroleum Company	**1979**	**1980**	**1981**	**1982**	**1983(I)**
Aramco	3,376.4	3,525.3	3,513.2	2,310.0	354.6
Getty Oil Co.	30.2	28.5	27.0	23.6	5.1
Arabian Oil Co.	72.6	70.0	45.6	33.4	5.6
Total	**3,479.2**	**3,623.8**	**3,585.8**	**2,367.0**	**365.3**
Total Average Daily Production (mbd)	9.52	9.90	9.82	6.48	4.06

Source: Saudi Arabian Monetary Agency Statistical Summary, 1983

Table 26.

SAUDI OIL CONCESSIONS

Company	**Area (sq km)**	**Year Awarded**	**Term**
Aramco	189,000* 31,000**	1933	66 years
Getty Oil Company	4,000* 1,000**	1949	60 years
Arabian Oil Company	3,400**	1960	40 years

*onshore
**offshore

Source: Middle East Economic Digest, July 1984

Table 27.

OIL EXPORTS BY COMPANY
(million bbl)

	1979	**1980**	**1981**	**1982**	**1983(I)**
Aramco (incl. Petromin)					
Crude	3,132.0	3,288.0	3,234.8	2,019.0	281.0
Refined	160.0	167.0	185.3	176.0	25.0
Getty					
Crude	19.2	20.6	19.5	10.1	1.4
Refined	10.1	7.3	5.2	13.2	3.5
Arabian Oil					
Crude	63.3	65.4	37.4	29.7	3.7
Refined	8.4	6.5	4.2	6.8	1.4
Total					
Crude	**3,214.5**	**3,374.0**	**3,291.7**	**2,058.8**	**286.1**
Refined	**178.5**	**180.8**	**194.7**	**196.0**	**29.9**

Source: Ministry of Petroleum, Central Department of Statistics

Table 28.

CRUDE PETROLEUM EXPORTS BY DESTINATION
(% of total)

	1978	1979	1980	1981	1982
North America					
Crude	18.10	19.94	18.34	15.44	8.31
Refined	.96	3.69	2.51	4.62	3.84
Latin America					
Crude	4.94	3.62	3.77	4.34	4.56
Refined	2.07	1.39	1.28	3.46	6.08
Western Europe					
Crude	38.83	41.55	42.43	42.43	35.35
Refined	8.92	11.86	20.47	26.16	17.28
Middle East					
Crude	3.47	3.24	2.92	3.48	3.74
Refined	.56	.68	1.04	3.74	5.06
Africa					
Crude	.49	.98	1.29	1.69	1.83
Refined	1.66	.81	.22	.13	--
Asia and Oceania					
Crude	34.25	30.68	31.24	32.60	46.21
Refined	58.98	58.44	57.00	52.22	61.76
Bunkers					
Refined	26.84	23.13	17.48	9.68	5.98
Total (million bbl)					
Crude	**2,812.696**	**3,218.468**	**3,375.694**	**3,291.537**	**2,058.392**
Refined	**178.356**	**178.343**	**180.434**	**194.892**	**196.094**

Source: Ministry of Petroleum and Mineral Resources

Table 29.

CRUDE OIL PRICES
(Dollars per Barrel)

Type of Crude/API Gravity	Price			
	1981	1982	1983	May 1984
Arabian Light 34° (Benchmark crude)	32.00	34.00	34.00	29.00
Saudi Berri 39°	33.52	35.40	34.52	29.52
Arabian Heavy 27°	31.00	31.00	31.00	26.00

Source: Weekly Petroleum Status Report/DOE May 24, 1984

Table 30.

PRODUCTION OF PETROLEUM PRODUCTS
(million bbl)

Product	1978	1979	1980	1981
Regular gasoline	6.7	6.6	7.8	7.7
Premium gasoline	13.0	14.7	19.0	24.5
LPG	65.3	79.5	74.9	69.5
Naphtha	48.3	51.3	45.5	38.9
Kerosene	9.9	9.9	11.7	12.0
Diesel oil	37.5	35.0	44.5	54.2
Fuel oil	95.4	98.0	89.0	85.5
Jet fuel	0.2	0.3	0.3	0.2
Other	7.3	9.5	9.7	12.0
Total	**283.6**	**304.7**	**302.4**	**304.5**
By Refinery				
Ras Tanura (Aramco)	232.8	248.2	251.9	240.0
Jeddah (Petromin)	21.6	30.1	30.9	29.5
Riyadh (Petromin)	5.4	7.4	5.4	24.3
Mina Saud (Getty Oil)	13.8	10.4	7.3	6.0
Ras al-Khafji (Arabian Oil)	10.0	8.6	6.9	4.7

Source: Ministry of Petroleum and Mineral Resources.

Table 31.

DOMESTIC CONSUMPTION OF REFINED PETROLEUM PRODUCTS
(million bbl)

	1976	1977	1978	1979	1980
Industrial fuels	31.565	47.607	58.077	81.657	119.096
Motor gasoline	12.934	16.640	20.145	24.412	31.869
Aviation gasoline	5.784	7.804	8.809	10.398	11.585
Kerosene	1.214	1.123	1.016	.904	1.266
Other	6.347	3.984	6.432	7.275	9.868
Total	**57.844**	**77.158**	**94.479**	**124.646**	**173.684**

Source: Ministry of Petroleum and Mineral Resources

Table 32.

ELECTRIC UTILITY INDUSTRY ENERGY SALES AND CONSUMPTION

	1979	1980	1981	1982
Residential				
Number of Customers	654,000	785,000	949,000	1,092,000
Energy Sales (GWH)	4,815	6,775	9,514	11,391
Consumption per Customer (KWH)	7,362	8,631	10,025	10,430
Non-Residential				
Number of Customers	73,000	87,000	93,000	121,000
Energy Sales (GWH)	8,634	10,662	12,129	15,240
Consumption per Customer (KWH)	118,274	122,552	130,419	125,709
Total Customers				
Number of Customers	727,000	872,000	1,042,000	1,213,000
Energy Sales (GWH)	13,449	17,437	21,643	26,631
Consumption per Customer (KWH)	18,499	19,997	20,771	21,955

Source: Saudi Arabian Monetary Agency Statistical Abstract, 1983

Table 33.

ELECTRIC UTILITY INDUSTRY PEAK LOAD AND INSTALLED CAPACITY

	1979	1980	1981	1982
Peak Load (MW)	2,955	3,986	5,227	6,309
Installed Capicity (MW)	4,124	5,904	7,359	9,001
Reserve (Capacity less Peak) (MW)	1,169	1,918	2,132	2,692
Reserve Margin (Reserve/Peak) (%)	39.6	48.1	40.8	42.7

Source: Saudi Industrial Development Fund Annual Report 1983

INDUSTRY

Table 34.

SABIC: DOMESTIC HEAVY INDUSTRY PROJECTS

Project	Signature Date	Site	Joint-Venture Partner	Products	Output 1000 tons/yr
Saudi Iron& Steel Co. (Hadeed)	3/79	Jubayl	DEG	Sponge iron,	800
				Steel billets,	850
				Steel rods & bars	800
		Jeddah		Steel rods & bars	140
Saudi Methanol Co. (Ar-Razi)	11/79	Jubayl	Japanese Consortium	Chemical grade methanol	600
National Methanol Co. (Ibn-Sina)	2/81	Jubayl	Celanese-Texas Eastern	Chemical grade methanol	650
Al-Jubayl Fertilizer Co. (Samad)	12/79	Jubayl	Taiwan Fertilizer Co.	Urea	500
Saudi Yanbu Petrochemical Co. (Yanpet)	4/80	Yanbu	Mobil	Ethylene	450
				Ethylene glycol	220
				Low-density polyethylene	200
				High-density polyethylene	90
Al-Jubayl Petrochemical Co. (Kemya)	4/80	Jubayl	Exxon	Polyethylene	260
Saudi Petrochemical Co. (Sadaf)	9/80	Jubayl	Shell Oil Co.	Ethylene	656
				Styrene	295
				Crude industrial ethanol	281
				Ethylene Dichloride	454
				Caustic soda	377
Arabian Petrochemical Co. (Petrokemya)	5/81	Jubayl	None	Ethylene	500
				Polyethylene	180
				Ethylene glycol	150
Eastern Petrochemical Co. (Sharq)	5/81	Jubayl	Japanese Consortium (SPDC)	Linear low-density polyethylene	130
				Ethylene glycol	300
Saudi Arabian Fertilizer Co. (Safco)	1964	Dammam	None	Urea	300
The National Gases Co.	1983	Jubayl	Seven Saudi gas companies	Oxygen	438
				Nitrogen	146

Source: Saudi Arabian Monetary Agency Statistical Summary, 1983

Table 35.

VALUE OF SIDF APPROVED INDUSTRIAL LOANS BY SECTOR
(million SR)

Sector	1979/80	1980/81	1981/82	1983/84
Food & Beverages	252	171	185	103
Textiles & Leathers	42	40	28	37
Wood Furniture & Carpentry Products	19	15	13	4
Paper Products & Printing	38	38	22	51
Chemicals	45	39	141	138
Oil & Gas Products	29	--	--	385
Rubber & Plastics	65	57	110	44
Ceramics & Glass	16	174	19	33
Cement	400	400	400	490
Other Building Materials	179	100	42	48
Metal Products	145	171	255	257
Machinery	80	30	20	20
Electrical Equipment	14	17	153	16
Transport Equipment	13	3	13	27
Other Manufacturing	2	4	15	9
Total	**1,339**	**1,259**	**1,415**	**1,663**

Source: Saudi Industrial Development Fund Annual Report, 1983

AGRICULTURE AND FISHING

Table 36.

AREA PLANTED AND PRODUCTION OF MAIN CROPS

(Production = thousand tons;
Area planted = thousand hectares;
Yield = tons per hectare.)

Crop	1977/78	1978/79	1979/80
Wheat			
Production	120	147	158
Area Planted	60	79	84
Yield	2.0	1.9	1.9
Sorghum			
Production	152	194	215
Area Planted	302	371	405
Yield	0.5	0.5	0.5
Barley			
Production	15	16	17
Area Planted	8	7	6
Yield	1.9	2.4	2.8
Millet			
Production	13	13	13
Area Planted	34	41	44
Yield	0.4	0.3	0.3
Tomatoes			
Production	167	212	218
Area Planted	16	20	21
Yield	10.7	10.6	10.3
Dry Onions			
Production	95	118	128
Area Planted	4	5	5
Yield	26.0	23.1	25.6

Sources: Central Dept of Statistics, Ministry of Finance and National Economy, Statistical Yearbook 1980, Saudi Arabian Monetary Agency Statistical Abstract, 1983

AREA PLANTED AND PRODUCTION OF MAIN CROPS

(Production = thousand tons;
Area planted = thousand hectares;
Yield = tons per hectare.)

Crop	1977/78	1978/79	1979/80
Eggplant			
Production	21	29	31
Area Planted	2	4	4
Yield	9.7	7.8	7.8
Watermelon			
Production	140	179	168
Area Planted	10	15	16
Yield	13.3	11.9	10.2
Dates			
Production	411	416	441
Area Planted	58	64	68
Yield	7.0	6.5	6.5
Grapes			
Production	56	53	57
Area Planted	4	6	6
Yield	12.8	9.5	9.2
Citrus Fruits			
Production	29	31	34
Area Planted	4	5	5
Yield	7.5	6.9	6.8

Table 37.
LIVESTOCK PRODUCT PRODUCTION, IMPORTS, CONSUMPTION
(Thousand tons)

	ACTUAL			PROJECTED	
	1978	1980	1982	1985	1990
Meat:					
Beef & Veal					
Production*	23	25	30	40	50
Imports	22	40	85	130	200
Consumption	45	65	115	170	250
Lamb & Mutton					
Production*	62	75	95	110	128
Imports	18	24	32	36	42
Consumption	64	99	127	146	170
Poultry					
Production*	20	50	105	165	225
Imports	128	193	270	330	380
Consumption	148	243	375	495	605
Other (Prepared & Preserved)					
Production	--	--	--	--	--
Imports	13	14	28	42	58
Consumption	13	14	28	42	58
Total Meat	**270**	**421**	**645**	**853**	**1,083**
Dairy Products:					
Butter					
Production	2	2	2	3	5
Imports	16	23	27	38	50
Consumption	18	25	29	40	55
Cheese					
Production	--	--	--	--	--
Imports	32	39	50	75	110
Consumption	32	39	50	75	110
Fresh Milk					
Production	210	224	310	340	390
Imports	30	36	45	60	70
Consumption	240	260	355	400	460
Nonfresh Milk					
Production	--	--	--	--	--
Imports	69	88	100	135	175
Consumption	69	88	100	135	175
Eggs					
Production	28	40	56	93	120
Imports	16	17	35	45	65
Consumption	36	57	91	138	185

* Production includes imported live animals slaughtered locally

Source: USDA: Foreign Agricultural Economic Report No. 182.

Table 38.

LIVE ANIMALS
(1000 head)

	ACTUAL			PROJECTED	
	1978	1980	1982	1985	1990
Cattle Imports	113	180	120	175	200
Poultry Imports	12,130	6,186	13,000	15,000	18,000
Sheep Imports	3,750	5,260	5,400	5,600	6,000

Source: USDA Foreign Economic Report No. 182

TRADE

Table 39.

BALANCE OF PAYMENTS
(million U.S. dollars)

	1979	1980	1981	1982
Merchandise Trade	**34,437**	**72,519**	**76,428**	**31,474**
Oil Exports	57,789	100,615	109,903	72,639
Other Exports	149	645	158	169
Imports	-23,501	-28,251	-33,633	-41,334
Services & Transfers	**-23,372**	**-31,091**	**-38,440**	**-30,174**
Receipts	**7,707**	**11,272**	**16,080**	**16,977**
Investment Income	4,908	7,446	10,851	11,624
Oil Sector	761	858	584	364
Other	2,037	2,967	4,644	4,988
Payments	**-31,079**	**-42,364**	**-54,521**	**-47,152**
Freight & Insurance	-3,994	-5,085	-6,054	-7,440
Oil Sector Investment Income	-2,063	-6,920	-9,508	-6,485
Other Private Services	-7,975	-6,645	-11,346	-8,581
Other Government Services	-13,685	-19,646	-23,533	-20,454
Private Transfers	-3,359	-4,066	-4,060	-4,190
Current Account Balance	**11,065**	**41,428**	**37,988**	**1,300**
Capital Movements & Reserves	**-11,065**	**-41,428**	**-37,988**	**-1,300**
Net Capital Transactions Including Oil Sector	-1,348	-3,197	+6,386	+5,815
Net Other Private Capital *	-6,904	-8,557	+3,810	+3,861
Net Commercial Banks	-1,557	-3,715	-6,212	-2,993
Official Capital & Reserves **	-1,253	-25,956	-41,972	-7,982
Exchange Rates Used:	3.365	3.325	3.415	3.435

* Includes inward direct investment, short-term private capital, valuation adjustment and net errors and omissions.

** Includes changes in total foreign assets of SAMA, i.e., gold, foreign exchange, and investments (including loans to developing countries).

Source: Saudi Arabian Monetary Agency Statistical Abstract, 1983

Table 40.

TRADE BY COMMODITY SECTOR
(% of total)

	1977	1978	1979	1980	1981
Exports					
Food	.1	.1	.1	.1	.1
Raw materials excluding fuel					
Fuels	99.7	99.2	99.1	99.2	99.3
Manufactured goods					
Imports					
Food	10.1	10.8	12.2	13.5	14.1
Raw Materials excluding fuel	2.2	1.8	2.0	2.3	1.8
Fuel	.6	.7	.6	.6	.7
Manufactured goods	86.3	86.7	84.9	83.1	83.2

Source: IFS Trade Statistics Supplement 1983

Table 41.

COMMODITY COMPOSITION OF IMPORTS
(million SR)

	1978	1979	1980	1981
Foodstuffs	7,802	10,511	14,192	17,279
Textiles & Clothing	4,178	4,996	6,571	7,294
Chemical Products	3,730	4,761	6,270	7,032
Cement	1,511	1,436	2,138	1,806
Wood, timber, wood articles	2,058	2,332	2,597	2,650
Jewelry, precious stones	1,659	1,304	2,397	3,478
Base metals & metal articles	9,588	12,730	14,611	17,443
Machinery, appliances, electrical equipment	19,844	22,552	24,534	30,323
Motor vehicles	5,562	6,940	9,535	9,670
Other transport eqpt.	3,474	4,052	4,389	7,572
Other commodities	9,774	10,609	13,116	14,751
Total	**69,180**	**82,223**	**100,350**	**119,298**

Sources: Central Dept of Statistics, Ministry of Finance and National Economy, Foreign Trade Statistics, and Saudi Arabian Monetary Agency (SAMA)

Table 42.

DIRECTION OF TRADE
(million U.S. dollars)

	EXPORTS			IMPORTS		
	1980	1981	1982	1980	1981	1982
World	**102,012**	**113,230**	**77,370**	**30,166**	**35,268**	**40,979**
Industrial Countries:	**76,941**	**81,799**	**49,879**	**24,023**	**28,420**	**33,773**
Australia	1,162	1,429	1,142	368	496	684
Belgium	3,716	2,886	1,608	473	518	703
Canada	2,021	2,018	218	137	165	262
France	9,434	10,799	6,746	1,635	2,023	2,159
Germany	3,104	4,748	3,532	2,739	3,369	4,299
Italy	6,276	8,032	3,657	2,208	2,368	2,595
Japan	17,805	19,436	18,258	5,411	6,456	7,687
Netherlands	6,966	6,321	2,778	955	931	1,001
Spain	2,974	3,709	2,116	542	576	549
United Kingdom	3,614	3,601	2,376	1,955	2,183	2,682
United States	15,796	15,179	5,751	6,040	7,559	8,989
Developing Countries:						
Oil Exporting Countries	**1,140**	**1,444**	**1,675**	**279**	**392**	**408**
Indonesia	991	1,022	1,196	11	34	34
Iran	4	12	6	20	35	28
Iraq	20	49	44	3	2	2
Kuwait	50	191	283	118	145	152
Libya	7	40	10	1	--	--
Oman	14	19	7	3	3	3
Qatar	15	23	33	63	76	83
United Arab Emirates	35	78	92	59	95	101
Non-Oil Exporters	**21,207**	**27,062**	**23,060**	**4,438**	**5,134**	**5,677**
Africa (total)	1,317	1,967	1,414	427	450	456
Asia (total)	10,819	13,500	12,786	2,310	2,695	3,139
Europe (total)	2,513	3,046	2,013	613	684	822
Middle East	3,184	4,112	3,301	735	933	827
Bahrain	2,012	2,544	2,123	90	161	185
Egypt	40	57	44	80	88	68
Jordan	382	549	620	122	140	107
Lebanon	392	381	185	375	379	334
Syria	11	285	57	59	158	126
Yemen Arab Republic	287	260	256	7	5	6
Yemen, P.D. Republic	60	38	16	2	3	2
Western Hemisphere(tot.)	3,324	4,098	3,330	221	248	307
USSR, Eastern Europe	**51**	**340**	**216**	**617**	**497**	**330**
Other	**1,047**	**1,125**	**819**	**211**	**156**	**128**

Source: IFS Trade Supplement, 1983

Table 43.

FOREIGN TRADE INDICATORS

	1977	1978	1979	1980	1981
Ratio of exports to imports	3.01	1.86	2.42	3.39	3.21
Ratio of imports to GDP	25.2	30.9	32.7	26.0	
Ratio of exports to GDP	75.7	57.6	79.1	87.9	
Terms of trade (IV quarter)	102.7	90.6	120.9	169.1	191.0

Source: IFS Trade Statistics Supplement, 1983

Table 44.

DIRECTION OF TRADE
(% of total trade)

	1977	1978	1979	1980	1981
Exports					
Industrial Countries	69.5	75.2	75.7	75.3	72.4
Oil Exporting Countries	.7	.8	1.1	1.1	1.3
Non-oil Developing Countries	23.2	20.2	20.3	20.8	23.9
Other Countries	6.6	3.7	2.9	2.8	2.4
Imports					
Industrial Countries	66.4	80.0	79.1	79.6	80.6
Oil Exporting countries	5.4	.9	1.4	.9	1.1
Non-oil Developing Countries	17.6	12.9	13.8	14.7	14.6
Other Countries	10.5	6.3	5.7	4.7	3.7

Source: IFS Trade Statistics Supplement, 1983

LABOR

Table 45.

EMPLOYMENT BY SECTOR

Sector	% of Economically Active Population* Employed
Agriculture	24.2
Mining	0.3
Oil and Refineries	1.5
Manufacturing	4.2
Public Utilities	1.3
Construction	13.3
Trade	12.6
Transport	8.7
Finance & Business Services	1.4
Community & Social Services	19.5
Public Adminstration & Defense	13.0

* Economically Active Population: 21% (2.2% women)

Source: Ministry of Planning estimates, 1982

Table 46.

DISTRIBUTION OF EMPLOYMENT BY ECONOMIC ACTIVITY
(Thousand Workers and Percent of Total)

	1974/75		1979/80	
	Workers	%	Workers	%
Producing sectors	988.6	56.6	1,107.9	44.8
Agriculture	695.0	39.8	598.8	24.2
Mining	3.4	0.2	7.3	0.3
Oil & refinerie	27.4	1.6	36.0	1.5
Manufacturing	74.4	4.2	104.2	4.2
Utilities	16.1	0.9	31.5	1.3
Construction	172.3	9.9	330.1	13.3
Service sectors	511.2	29.3	1,942.3	42.2
Trade	153.6	8.8	310.6	12.6
Transport	114.5	6.5	214.6	8.7
Finance & business services	13.1	0.8	34.8	1.4
Community & social services	230.0	13.2	482.3	19.5
Goverment (civilian)	246.7	14.1	321.0	13.0
Total	**1,746.5**	**100.0**	**2,471.2**	**100.0**

Average annual growth rate of labor force: 3.5% (1970-80)

Source: Ministry of Planning

Table 47.

CIVILIAN EMPLOYMENT IN SAUDI ARABIA
(Thousands)

Nationality/sex	1979/80	1984/85*	Net Change	Annual Growth Rate (%)
Saudi men	1,308.4	1,437.4	+129.0	1.9
Non-Saudi men	1,014.9	1,023.9	+9.0	0.2
Total men	2,323.3	2,461.3	+138.0	1.2
Saudi women	103.0	120.0	+17.0	3.1
Non-Saudi women	44.9	44.9	--	--
Total women	147.9	164.9	+17.0	2.2
Total Saudis	1,411.4	1,557.4	+146.0	1.9
Total Non-Saudis	1,059.8	1,068.8	+9.0	0.2
Grand Total	**2,471.2**	**2,626.2**	**+155.0**	**1.2**

* projected

Source: Third Development Plan (1980-85), Ministry of Planning

Table 48.

COMPOSITION OF THE LABOR FORCE
(in 1980 figures)

North Yemen	600,000
Egypt	300,000
Pakistan	200,000
Jordan/Palestinians	100,000
South Korea	80,000
Phillipines	70,000
UK/USA	30,000
TOTAL	**1,380,000**

Source: Foreign Policy Association, 1984; Economist Intelligence Unit, Annual Supplement, 1983

TRANSPORTATION AND COMMUNICATIONS

Table 49.

TRANSPORTATION INFRASTRUCTURE

Km of railroad: 747
Ports: Jeddah, Dammam, Yanbu, Jizan, Jubayl
National airline: Saudia
Airports: Riyadh Int'l, Dhahran Int'l, Damman, Jeddah Int'l
# of airfields: 101- 81 usable, 23 with permanent surface runways, 15 with runways over 2,500 m

Source: MERI

Table 50.

SAUDIA'S FLEET

	Owned	Leased	On order
Boeing 747			10
Lockheed L-1011	16		
Airbus Industrie A300		2	11
Boeing 707	6		
Boeing 737	19		
McDonnell Douglas DC8		7	
Fokker F-28		2	
Beechcraft A100	2		
Cessna 421B	1		
Grumman Gulfstream 11	4		
Piper PA23	2		

Source: MEED Special Report on Saudi Arabia, July 1981

Table 51.

VOLUME OF PASSENGERS AT INTERNATIONAL AIRPORTS
(million)

	1978	1979	1980	1981	1982
Jeddah	4,875	6,648	7,505	7,270	7,798
Riyadh	3,642	4,415	5,279	5,302	5,959
Dhahran	2,279	2,665	3,305	3,685	4,362

Source: Saudi Business April 16, 1984

Table 52.

TOURISM

Pilgrims to Mecca From Abroad

1975/76	894,573
1976/77	719,040
1977/78	739,319
1978/79	830,236
1979/80	862,520
1980/81	812,892
1981/82	879,368
1982/83	853,555

Source: Saudi Arabian Monetary Agency Statistical Summary, 1983

Table 53.

TOTAL CARGO AT THE INTERNATIONAL AIRPORTS
(metric tons)

	1978	1979	1980	1981	1982
Jeddah	32,908	48,041	62,556	77,178	103,030
Riyadh	21,104	27,639	30,391	43,465	65,565
Dhahran	17,134	28,176	36,021	49,466	72,769

Source: Saudi Business April 16, 1984

Table 54.

PORTS AND SHIPPING

	1977	1978	1979	1980
Port Development				
Number of Berths at all seaports	53	75	95	101
Handling Capacity (thousand tons)*	17,850	21,530	31,100	37,800
Volume of Crude Petroleum and Petroleum Products Loaded by Ports (mn b/d)				
Ras Tanura	3,259	2,901	3,291	3,455
Al-Khafji	37	61	77	73
Mina Saud	32	29	30	28
Total	**3,328**	**2,991**	**3,398**	**3,556**
Volume of Import Cargo Unloaded by Ports (thousand weight tons)				
Jeddah	8,447	9,979	12,527	13,965
Dammam	6,568	7,686	8,739	9,178
Yanbu	850	726	1,075	1,335
Jizan	550	663	1,049	1,494
Jubail	---	849	954	1,508
Total	**16,415**	**19,903**	**24,344**	**27,480**

*Calculated at 70% Occupancy

Source: Ports Authority & Ministry of Petroleum & Natural Resources, 1982

Table 55.

TELEPHONES IN THE KINGDOM
(thousand)

	1976/77	1977/78	1978/79	1979/80	1980/81
Exchange Line Capacity	134.6	182.0	215.0	397.9	587.3
Number of Operating Telephones	108.1	126.0	156.8	227.3	319.6

Source: Central Department of Statistics and Ministry of PTT, 1983

Table 56.

PRINCIPAL DAILY NEWSPAPERS

Newspaper	Circulation
Arab News (English)	n.a.
al-Bilad (Arabic)	30,000
al-Jazirah (Arabic)	105,000
al-Madina al-Munawara (Arabic)	30,000
al-Nadwah (Arabic)	10,000
Okaz Newspaper (Arabic)	80,000
al-Riyadh (Arabic)	140,000
Saudi Gazette (English) Business daily	n.a.
Saudi Review (English) Daily newsletter from Saudi newspapers and broadcasting service	5,000
al-Yaum (Arabic):	42,000

Source: MERI

Table 57.

RADIO AND TELEVISION BROADCASTING

TV stations: The Saudi Arabian Government Television Service has twelve transmitters at:

Riyadh	Jeddah	Medina
Dammam	Qassim	Abha
Hail	Al-baha	Sakaka
Al-Qurayat	Wadiadda-Wasir	Tabuk

SAGTS broadcasts 8 hours per day.

Aramco Television is based in Dhahran and is non-commercial. Broadcasts 4.5 hours per day.

# of radio receivers: 310,000 (1982)
# of television receivers: 3.1 million (1982)

Sources: MERI

HEALTH, EDUCATION AND WELFARE

Table 58.

HEALTH FACILITIES IN THE KINGDOM

	1977/78	1978/79	1979/80	1980/81
Number of Hospitals, Dispensaries, Clinics, etc.	1,071	1,138	1,180	1,283
Hospitals				
Number	99	102	98	104
Number of Beds	13,346	13,745	15,102	17,523
Medical & Para-Medical Personnel				
Physicians	4,075	4,556	5,130	6,461
Nursing Staff	8,359	8,700	10,278	12,255
Technical Assistants	4,440	4,749	5,355	6,524

Source: Ministry of Health

Table 59.

ENROLLMENT IN EDUCATIONAL INSTITUTIONS
(% of total population)

	1977	1978	1979	1980
Primary School Enrollment Ratio				
Total	58.0	60.0	62.0	64.0
Female	44.0	46.0	48.0	51.0
Secondary School Enrollment Ratio				
Total	26.0	28.0	30.0	30.0
Female	19.0	21.0	22.0	24.0
Vocational Enrollment (percentage of Secondary School Enrollment)	1.7	1.4	1.4	1.5
Pupil-Teacher Ratio				
Primary	18.0	19.0	18.0	18.0
Secondary	14.0	13.0	13.0	13.0
Adult Literacy Rate	--	--	--	24.6

Source: World Bank, Social Data, 1983

Table 60.

SCHOOLS, TEACHERS AND PUPILS IN SAUDI ARABIA

1980/81	Schools	Teachers	Pupils
Kindergarten	195	1114	28,045
Elementary	5,744	50,010	930,436
Intermediate	1,539	16,768	256,724
Secondary	513	5,962	100,023
Adult	2,991	7,958	136,103
Higher	55*	6,598	56,252
Special	58	862	1,971
Technical	30	903	6,920

*Faculties

Source: Ministry of Education